The Lucky Bean Tree

Pamela McFarlane

Copyright © 2018 Pamela McFarlane

All rights reserved, including the right to reproduce this book, or portions thereof in any form. No part of this text may be reproduced, transmitted, downloaded, decompiled, reverse engineered, or stored, in any form or introduced into any information storage and retrieval system, in any form or by any means, whether electronic or mechanical without the express written permission of the author.

The views expressed in this work are solely those of the author and do not necessarily reflect the views of the publisher, and the publisher hereby disclaims any responsibility for them.

ISBN: 978-0-244-71929-6

Dedicated to Richard John Bebb

04.05.1987-06.08.2016

'Write a book, Mother!' he said.
So I did.

Beginnings

I was a mistake. A shock. Conceived one month after the birth of my brother I like to think I am the surprise gift that just keeps on giving. My mother Barbara had returned home to my dad, Jim, a legendary foxy Lethario, three weeks after the birth. Not one to dally in matters of the heart, it was wham, bam, thank you ma'am! And there I was, swimming in organic soup, raining on my brother's parade.

My first memories are hazy. Born in Salisbury, Rhodesia – now Harare, Zimbabwe – my first recollections are of Cape Town, where we moved when my brother, David and I were still very young. My sister Jenny was born in Cape Town, four years after my birth.

We lived in a double storey house in Milnerton and this is where I discovered that God lived under my bed. Going to bed as a three-year-old was scary. My bedroom was on the first floor and the downstairs lounge, where my parents tried to relax after a long day, seemed very far away at bed-time. At first, I thought it was the dreaded Bogeyman who lived under my bed. If my hands trailed down the side of the bed I knew he would grab my arm and start eating me, fingers first. Getting into bed was a nightmare too so I leapt onto my bed from as far away as possible so the Bogeyman couldn't grab my leg. He was partial to toes.

One day I just clicked. There was no Bogeyman. God lived under my bed. He was kind and he didn't fancy eating digits of any kind so I allowed Him to stay.

After nearly three years in Cape Town, my family moved to Durban North, Natal, where my brother Peter was born. Six years younger than me he was the apple of everyone's eye. He got away with murder from infancy because he was so squishy and squeezable. He was the original Cabbage Patch Doll. Our family was now complete.

We lived in a cul-de-sac, on one side of the Japanese Gardens valley. David and I played 'gangs' in the valley with the neighbourhood kids. Actually, he played and I tagged along, a chubby, annoying little sister who was no good at climbing mango trees and chasing imaginary forest creatures. In one particular episode of gang warfare a mean seven-year old from the other gang threw a brick straight at my chest, winding me. I sported a beautiful brick-shaped bruise that turned purple-blue for some weeks. I wore it with pride. I was a bona-fida Valley Gang member. I belonged.

The only other vivid memory I have of the time in Durban was the day a strange woman gave birth to a bottle of brandy in our house.

The strange woman knocked on our door on a Saturday morning and my parents let her into the lounge where she lowered herself slowly into an armchair and crossed her legs. My parents and I sat opposite her on the settee. I was fascinated by her speech. She slurred and hiccupped and giggled as she tried to have a conversation with my parents. Then, as we watched in awe, a bottle of brandy started slithering slowly out of her dress, neck first. It exited from her unmentionable place, squeezed past her thighs and hugged her knees before plopping onto the carpet. It was a surreal moment. I felt congratulations were in order but my parents threw her out forthwith.

After Durban we moved to Johannesburg for one year then moved back to Cape Town. It was like playing relocation ping-pong.

This time we lived in Constantia, near forests, veld and vineyards, in a single storey home with our mongrel dog, Tippy. One of our family traditions was listening to Squad Cars on Springbok Radio every Friday night. My parents, David and I hunkered around our vinyl-topped kitchen table and listened with rapt attention.

They prowl the empty streets at night –waiting. In fast cars, on foot, living with crime & violence. These men are on duty 24 hours out of every 24. They face dangers at every turn, expecting nothing less. They protect the people of South Africa – These are the men of Squad Cars!

https://archive.org/details/SquadCars

Life was carefree and my siblings and I spent hours in the veld, taking aim at unsuspecting birds with pellet guns, picking sour grapes off the vines and searching for snakes. My mother was not quite as carefree for much of our time here. This was the first time I noticed she was depressed although I didn't know the word. She spent the mornings in bed when we were at school then pottered around the house sadly during the afternoons. However, something happened when I was ten years old that shook her, quite literally, out of her state of lethargy.

The 29th of September, 1969, was an auspicious date. It was 8:00pm and I was in my bedroom asleep when the earth groaned loudly and moved underneath us. My cupboards started jumping around and leaning perilously towards my bed, which was dancing clumsily across the floor with me inside it. My parents came running in and yelled at us all to get out into the garden. Minutes later four pyjama-clad children and two wild-eyed adults were in the front garden, panic-struck. We didn't sleep very much that night.

I went to Sweet Valley Primary School in Bergvliet, Cape Town. This is where I met my first very best friend, Kate. I adored her. I wanted to be like her. She was strong and blonde and beautiful. She was a child of the universe with eyes that seemed to know the mysteries of life. She could do everything well, especially sporty stuff. I was the opposite. I was bookish and self-conscious and preferred reading to physical exertion. I was the kid who was always picked last for PE sporting teams. School sports days were nightmare occasions for me, even though I was usually put into the relay race or the potato sack race. I did, however excel at the three-legged race if teamed up with another child of my size. It did not look pretty but running as a two-humped beast seemed to suit me. Sprinting was an ideal I never reached. I always seemed to be drawn against Carol Glanville, a muscular, tanned girl with hair like straw and freckles splattered across her nose, who flew like the wind down the race track. I was lost before I had begun. My father, a natural athlete, yelled from the sidelines, in the vain hope that would increase my capabilities. During one sports day he was totally embarrassed by another father (probably Carol Glanville's dad) who yelled in frustration – We always have the slow ones! – as I trundled along to the finish line in defeat. He never admitted to being my father.

My sporty friend Kate ended up sailing solo across the Atlantic. She also skippered Foschini Girl, an all-female yacht crew, who sailed from Cape Town to Rio. She is like a female Bear Grylls and still, to this day, challenges herself physically and mentally to do the impossible. She is one of my heroes.

I first felt the stirrings of love when I was about nine, a year before the earthquake. My parents had good friends who lived in Milnerton and we often went to visit them and their two children. Their home was ruled by cats and gnomes. Cats lived in the butter, on the stove, on the beds and on the telephone. They draped themselves over armrests, available human heads and over the gnomes. The gnomes lived in the back garden. What is the collective noun for gnomes? The internet offers up: an annoyance, a picnic, a half-pint, an army, a lawn, a gnope of gnomes. At any rate, there were hundreds, planted around ponds, hidden in hedging, lurking behind bushes and lining the pathways like evil hobgoblins.

My love was at least eleven, devastatingly handsome and a complete moron when it came to girlish crushes. To be fair, his hormones had not yet fully kicked in and dealing with a frizzy-haired, moonfaced, love-struck pre-adolescent must have been tricky. The gnomes were more appreciative of my devotion and far less annoying.

Another kind of infatuation was going on over this time. Father Christmas came to visit with us many times at this cat-gnome home.

I was a very young girl, my body not yet fully grown, when a jovial, welcoming chap who played Father Christmas for the community every festive season determined to share his particular form of festive cheer with me in the most unseasonal times and in a most unseasonable way. This family friend, who socialized with my parents and the gnome-owners, over the course of time unwrapped me layer by layer, like a longed-for Christmas present, stripping bare my defences and rendering me mute.

His whispered comfort – 'trust me' – confused and placated me at the same time. I knew I was very special. I knew I was very bad.

It was about this time I realised I could get behind someone's eyes and look through them, see the world as they saw it. It was a strange talent and I didn't do it very often, only when I couldn't understand what was happening and I needed to feel safe. So I went behind my mother's eyes and tried to make her see. She did not. No-one saw.

I told her and my dad when I was forty years old, sitting in their retirement home in Randburg as this man was shown on the TV news. He'd been brought to justice after molesting hundreds of young girls over the years. James McNeil, dubbed the Father Christmas paedophile, aged seventy-five, was sentenced to ten years in 2003, of which five were conditionally suspended for five years. My silence was broken.

Plucked out of Cape Town when I was in my penultimate year at primary school, we relocated to Bulawayo, Rhodesia. I was convinced God had orchestrated this, to save me from further fawning affections of Father Christmas. It was a magic answer to unspoken prayers.

Bulawayo

I started my final year of primary school at Tennyson Primary after relocating from Cape Town. Our class was like a packet of liquorice allsorts, an odd assortment of kids who were typically pre-adolescent in shape - either fat, skinny, lanky, broad or stumpy, which suited me fine as I was a round little sun-burnt butterball and I fitted right in with this motley crew.

My one beauty (with apologies to Louisa May Alcott) was my brain. I was clever. However I met my nemesis in a doe-eyed fairy-child called Morna. She was so beautiful, so delicate and annoyingly clever. We vied for top spot throughout the year and I'm jolly sure she came out on top but I acted like I had been the academic victor.

My sporting prowess was still hopeless and I hated running around the playing field as the boiling hot African sun fried my face, turning it deep crimson as I exercised. My outstanding achievement was being knocked unconscious during a game of Red Rover. After Red Rover was called, I tucked my head into my shoulders and steamed straight across the gap between the two teams like a bull who had spied a red flag. However all I could see was the sun-scorched grass of the field and not the approaching member of the other team. He was likewise oblivious to oncoming traffic and we connected heads with a loud bang. We passed out simultaneously. I earned myself a bit of street-cred that day.

We lived at 13 Beryl Drive, Beacon Hill, a wealthy suburb at the top of a very steep, winding hill. Our house was a split-level, modern 60's build, placed within an acre of grounds. We had a gravel tennis court surrounded by scarlet bougainvillea and a swimming pool enclosure with a kidney-shaped pool. There was a wondrous giant boulder hugging the kidney curve which we used as a launching pad to jump off into the water. We had servants for every conceivable need, pawpaw trees, rose gardens and a lucky bean tree. Life was not too shabby.

I loved sitting on the shady rockery underneath the lucky bean tree. My friends were the colourful chameleons that skittered along tree branches and over hot rocks. I sat quietly, watching, as they stopped moving, claimed their spot and blended in with their surroundings. My skin was a deep brown, thanks to the ever-burning sunshine. This created a canvas for my artistic works as I drew pictures all over my arms and legs with a sharp twig right onto my leathery, tanned skin. My eraser was my spit-covered hands, which I used to wipe the pictures off, ready for the next creative artwork.

The lucky bean tree was my own special cathedral. Surrounded by leaves that filtered the sun, ensconced by jagged rocks, hidden from view, I found my safe place. In springtime, my cathedral flowered blood-red, poker blooms, creating a sacred crypt. My glass rosary beads reflected sunshine and crimson streaks as I held it against the dappled light. My favourite time under my tree was near Christmas time, when the tree's black pods formed and hung down towards the ground. I knew then that lucky beans would soon be released. Once dry, the pods burst, scattering their riches on the earth below. Bright coral-red coloured beans with a black patch on one end, as if dipped in paint, adorned my crypt and the surrounding garden beds.

My parents threw tennis parties on weekends in the late afternoons, when the fierce heat of the sun lessened and long shadows from bordering trees cooled the gravel. The guests and my parents wore tennis whites, frilly tennis panties being part of the gear for the women. They carried their wooden tennis racquets in frames, which kept them from warping. I was horrified to discover that English olde-worlde shops now have these racquets from my childhood in their window displays. My childhood sports equipment is now considered antique. Quite what that makes me, I shudder to think.

All of us children had to be ball-boys. Gender misappropriation was not a matter of social conscience back then. The adult players therefore had a very leisurely game as we did all the running and sweating on their behalf. When they say down in the pergola under the shade of bougainvillea, we served them drinks then sat down ourselves to eat juicy oranges cut into quarters.

Having Sundowners was a Colonial habit. Most evenings between five and six o'clock the adults gathered in the cool of the lounge to indulge in chatter, cigarettes and liquor. Every good Colonial home had a Liquor Cabinet, locked with a key and opened for times such as these. Once the cabinet was opened, the door formed a shelf upon which all manner of drinks were mixed. My father usually did the honours. His mother, my Granny Katie, adored brandy with a splash of milk. My mother's favourite tipple was brandy and coke whilst my father had a special relationship with whisky. However there was a vast array of other alcoholic treats to cater for every visitor's tastes.

As we were children we were allowed soft drinks only. However, we were left to tidy it all away when the adults repaired to the dining room or to the balcony to soak up the hot night air and continue their verbal discourse. This was our moment. We slurped the dregs of every glass, licked the bottom of leaking bottles and sucked the fag-ends of smoked cigarettes. Dizzy with this smoky, boozy cocktail, we toddled quickly out the lounge before we got caught.

My father was a successful businessman but he was under the misapprehension that he had another talent, that of growing vegetables. We had a full-time gardener, described in those Colonial days as a 'garden boy' even though he was over fifty. He looked after our acre of gardens beautifully and he also grew some vegetables behind the servants' quarters to add to the servants' rations. Not to be outdone, my father decided to bring out his latent farming genes and started to grow cauliflowers.

Our family sat down at the dining room table every evening for dinner. Our houseboy, John, laid the table beforehand, leaving a little bell just near my mother's plate. When we were all at table and ready to eat, she rang the little bell and John came in with the first course. On the days we knew we were eating cauliflower in any form, I started gagging at the first ring of the bell. My father had perfected raising giant cauliflowers that looked wonderful. On closer inspection however, within the undulating folds of caulie, there resided a mega-city of aphids.

My father refused to acknowledge these beasties as inedible and made us eat the crunchy black dots saying they were protein and we should be grateful. We rejoiced when the caulie crop eventually died out and my father's passion for agricultural cultivation was exchanged for a passion for Petula Clark records which kept him indoors.

Our property had a frog pond at the bottom of the sweeping drive. Made from rocks, it created a haven for all of Bulawayo's frogs. It was like a time-share for local and travelling amphibians and boy, could these holiday makers party! The sound was indescribable. It leaked into every room in the house, echoing over the parquet flooring and bouncing off the walls. Something needed to be done. The children were given a mission, should we choose to accept it. And it wasn't collecting tadpoles and lovingly watch them grow into frogs. It was less Mission Impossible, more The Terminator.

The pond was backed by a four-foot high wall which we used, together with the long-handled swimming pool net, as a weapon of mass destruction.

All four of us took turns in spotting, scooping, hurling and counting. The net was used to scoop up the croaking frog; the perpetrator then swung the net pole back as far back as he or she could and whipped it around to fling the startled frog against the stone wall. The winner was the one whose frog made the loudest splat on the wall. Bulawayo was not a hive of cultural amusements or sophistication.

We did however, have The Eskimo Hut, a drive-in restaurant near the Royal Academy of Music. After our weekly lessons in piano and music theory, my mother took us to the Eskimo Hut for ice-cream. The Valiant was so wide it could take three kids and my mother all in the front seat. Her out-flung arm was the emergency seat belt. At times of impending doom the kids in the front would be nearly decapitated and the kid at the back would shoot into the back of the front seat and crumple with a whimper into a heap in the back foot well.

There was another activity on offer in this Colonial backwater. Modelling and Deportment courses were run for teenage girls. This was necessary to try to make ladies of us, girls who played barefoot in dusty African soil way after we were considered to be little children. The Holy Grail was Posture and this was exceedingly Important. It was so Important it was Imperative and required Capitalization when printed on the Modelling and Deportment Pamphlet. As my usual walk was round-shouldered with my knuckles dragging on the floor, I was considered an ideal candidate for this course.

So I learned how to walk upright on the runway, eyes forward, chin up, tummy in, smiling serenely. I still managed to look fairly simian as I did so but at least I wore nice clothes. My mother, despite being married to a wealthy man, insisted on buying us clothes from Cash Wholesalers and shoes from the Bata factory shop. A few girls in the 'in' crowd at school actually referred to me in earshot as the girl 'who was ugly and her mother dresses her funny.'

No longer. I was a Model. I did the final exam, which was judged during a fashion show put on for all our parents. I stalked on, following the route of an imaginary line, legs criss-crossing sexily (in my mind) as I surveyed the audience with a haughty look. Stride. Stop. Pose. Stride. Turn. Pose. Stride. Remember Posture! Pose. Stride. Exit. Whip off day wear and adorn yourself with evening wear. Stalk. Stride. Stop. Pose. Repeat.

We all passed, mainly because our parents had paid for the course and needed results. As soon as it had ended, I relaxed my tummy muscles and sloped out of the venue clutching my certificate.

At the time my modelling career began I was at the point of ending my dancing career. I had done ballet since I was a knee-high. It was supposed to help with deportment but as can be seen from my modelling abilities it had clearly not worked. I loved dressing up for shows in tutus and sequins. Looking back at old photos, however, reminds me of the time I danced in a kiddie version of Swan Lake when I was nine and still living in Cape Town. Dancing as a cygnet does not reflect my inelegant version of this classic, so it's more accurate to say I danced as a baby swan – lots of wing-flapping and legs like little egg-beaters churning away under the tutu. What I found most upsetting - and I remember this clearly - was that my head-dress resembled nothing other than a giant old-fashioned sanitary napkin with both end-loops hooked around my ears.

As I had recently made acquaintance with my mother's stack of monthly delights and the indescribable purpose for which she said they were used, I felt humiliated. No baby swan should endure such embarrassment.

My heroine was Margot Fonteyn. She was also my kindred spirit. I knew this because we both had the same toes. Our big toes are gigantic and the others are all half the size, like a row of cocktail sausages next to a frankfurter. This made pointe work extremely tricky and Margot suffered greatly in her journey of becoming a prima ballerina. I embraced the struggle until I was fourteen. My body shape was not conducive to ballet. My centre of gravity was my bust. I had no waist and my thighs rubbed together in my tights, causing static. (On one occasion I was convinced there were sparks flying from below my tutu. I did feel terrifyingly hot down below).

My teacher called out regularly – pull your stomach IN! – an instruction I followed with all my might. The day I gave up ballet was the day she yelled this at me for the third time that lesson and I yelled back venomously – I AM!

I tried modern dance for a year after that as I could get away with being a little interpretive. Yes, I am supposed to do a back bend and collapse on the floor, can't you see my fingers reaching artistically behind my head as I emerge like a butterfly from my chrysalis? Yes, starfish IS a modern dance position. Yes, leaping around the floor with arms flapping in time to the music is a legitimate expression of flight. It was so frustrating that no one could interpret my dancing. It crushed my spirit and I tried horse-riding instead.

There was one popular Bulawayo stable to which most parents sent their children to be taught all things equestrian. I don't know where the owner got his horses from but there were definitely horses there with additional emotional needs. They were as grumpy as can be and downright cranky most of the time. I was a bit scared of them, particularly when they bared their hideous teeth and blew hot smelly breath in my face. When they accompanied this by a demented whinny I lost all my composure. We had to wear our hard helmet hats and jodhpurs. I won't even go into what wearing jodhpurs did to my self-esteem. I shall leave that topic to rest.

I could manage sitting on the horse whilst it walked. Trotting was another matter. Again, my bosoms played a major part in my sporting ability. Even in my young teen years they had a life of their own and trotting confused them utterly. They did not know which way to bounce. They did not bounce in unison nor did they bounce with any sense of decorum. At the same time, my bottom hit the saddle in total discord with the rhythm of the trot, my feet turned out like panic flares and my chin juddered uncontrollably under my helmet strap. I was not a natural rider.

I will get ahead of myself here. I rode (sat on a walking horse) a few times in my adult years and when I was forty I went to one of the game reserves in South Africa that offered horse-riding safaris. This was the stuff of holiday brochures; holiday makers riding horses past dozy giraffes and skitterish bucks as the sun set over the African savannah, painting the distant mountains deep purple. I chose the four hour safari and was helped onto my horse by a laughing groom.

We set off into the grassy plains, hearing nothing but the sound of horses neighing softly and bird calls ringing in the air. There were twelve in our party and I was placed at the end. Presumably this was so a lion would be able to catch an easy meal, like jungle fast food – I'll have the Big Jiggly Lump on Horse please! We walked along small trails, making the most of shade from thorn trees, keeping our eyes peeled for wild game. We passed a tower of giraffe, their legs in touching distance which perturbed me somewhat. With one little kick of a hoof I could be in orbit so I urged my steed ahead, wanting to avoid space travel at that time.

I felt genuine panic when we drew close to a mother rhino and her baby. Not to worry! – was the rallying cry from our guide. Rhinos cannot see very well! Relax! Let us go closer and test that theory! See? They cannot see us! This is such fun! We are so close we can see the wrinkles in their armour-plated skin! Oh, the wonder of an African safari! Then the mother looked up. Myopically, she stared at us with her beady little eyes. We could be trees. Then her cup-like ears started waving around like antenna trying to find a signal. Her rhino nose started twitching. She stamped her foot, raising a cloud of red dust. She knew we were not trees. The guide started backing his horse away very slowly, showing us by the rolling whites of his eyes that we were to do the same.

By the time we got back from our ride I was numb. We had to park our horse next to a sort of shelf and then clamber over this and drop down on the other side. After riding for four hours my legs were fused to the body of the horse. I could not lift them off the saddle. My body was locked into a John Wayne position and refused to co-operate. It took two burly grooms to heave me off my horse and place me on the ground. I retained my John Wayne posture for some time in situ. I could not conceive of walking ever again. Eventually, I hobbled wretchedly to our rondawel, riding an invisible horse and emitting shrieks of pain with every move.

Back in Bulawayo, my entertainment in my early teens comprised of watching electric storms from my bedroom window, settling down to watch Bonanza on Friday nights, with dinner in our laps – an unheard of privilege – and going to church youth groups.

My family had a hodge-podge of spiritual traditions. My grandmother taught me how to read tea-leaves, back in the day when people drank tea with loose leaves. My mother read palms – my wrinkled, old-woman's palms were a challenge and a delight to read – and most of our relatives 'saw dead people'. My parents were part of the Methodist church, my brother was dedicated in the Spiritualist Church and some family members belonged to the Elim Pentecostals. We were a veritable faith fruit salad. I often retreated to my lucky bean tree crypt to ponder these things.

The dead people thing caused great anxiety within me, as did some of the other practices of the Spiritualist beliefs. I was encouraged to learn how to read a crystal ball, which didn't come naturally to me so a career at the local funfair was out of the question. My grandmother did praise me however, when I drew faces. I was quite a good artist and loved drawing people, particularly portraits. She was adamant that I was drawing spirit guides and long-dead people who had a message for me. It was a fairly common occurrence in our family to see spirits standing behind a chair, sitting on the end of a bed or peeking through the window.

When I was twelve, I was sent to stay with my grandmother and step-grandfather for a short holiday in the teeny tiny town of Dett which lay about three hundred kilometres north-west of Bulawayo.

Dett was a small yet important railway depot, and my step-grandfather who worked for Rhodesia Railways, was stationed there for a period of time.

I enjoyed my hot and sticky days there, making mountains of marshmallows with my granny and cooking up all sorts of other sweet delights. I dreaded the nights. Even though my granny didn't speak about spooky stuff to me while I was there I knew she still saw dead people and it terrified me. For all I knew, they all came to visit at night time and had a ghostly shindig in the lounge. After my evening bath I shot as fast as possible across the wooden floor and leapt on my bed quickly, before any spirit got too familiar. It was almost impossible to sleep in my state of fear. Every noise I heard, from gurgling pipes to tree branches tapping on the window, made my bones turn to stone. They were there. And they were coming to get me.

Another home I loved visiting was that of my mother's sister, Aunty Trudy. She also saw dead people and frequently had long chats with them. When I spent time there I looked over my shoulders, bug-eyed, if I heard an unexpected scrape of a chair or saw a curtain suddenly flutter in a breeze. She told me I was psychic and encouraged me to embrace my gift. I got as far as reading tea-leaves in the bottom of a cup, still my only spiritualistic party trick. As previously mentioned,

I could never see anything in a crystal ball. I concentrated so hard during every attempted reading that my eyes crossed and started watering.

Aunty Trudy had been a child-bride, like my mother, when she married my Uncle Fred. They quickly had a gang of kids, three girls, Tracy, Charmaine and Julie as well as Wayne, the only boy and we became close cousins. They had very little money and very few possessions but bucket-loads of love and laughter soaked their home. My aunty and my cousins were free spirits, unfettered by social pressures and the need to impress anyone else, no matter how important these people thought they might be. They lived life in the moment. When there was money, they partied! When there was none, they made cake.

Uncle Fred worked for Coca Cola so there was always a treasure trove of Coke in their house. Part of their energy was as a result of imbibing rivers of black, bubbly, liquid sugar. They were happy. They were quite probably high.

If I could Instagram a snapshot of their family today, I'd put six hyper-active puppies into a woven bamboo basket, fill the remaining space with butterflies, friendly ghosts, a colourful assortment of unicorns and top the lot with a glorious rainbow. #freefamily#bubblyblackriver#friendlyghost#loveinabamboobasket.

My Uncle John was also a spiritualist by all accounts. He had shrugged off his poor family background and become a successful businessman. His second wife, Aunty Marion, was always beautifully made up and very softly spoken, a real lady. In my early teens I learned that it took effort for her to look that good. Aunty Marion got up at 5:30 every morning to bath and prepare for the day. I was well impressed. My two cousins, Craig and Leanne, were also always beautifully turned out and immeasurably polite. They were the opposite side of the family coin to the rest of us.

Once when I was visiting them I helped Aunty Marion prepare dinner. 'Have you ever had tongue?' she asked me. I was most alarmed. I wondered aloud what kind of tongue she was talking about. When I heard it was a cow's tongue I thought she was having a laugh. So I peered into the pot on the stove and blow me down, there was a giant, fat, pink tongue boiling away gently. My stomach heaved. My legs went from beneath me when she hauled it out of the pot and PEELED it. Somewhere in the farmland near Bulawayo was a cow without a tongue, unable to even moo her objection properly.

We ate it for dinner with mash and a mustard sauce, I seem to remember. Peeled cow tongue with mustard. Who'd have thought something so gross could be so friggin' tasty? It remains one of my favourite meats to this day.

My mother's youngest brother, Denis, was a dead-people-speaker as well. His second wife, Helen, was a no-nonsense tough cookie who didn't care if dead people spoke to her as long as they listened and did what she told them to do. They had four children and brought them up pretty much like Baron von Trapp of Sound of Music fame. Like my Aunty Trudy and her family, they too had very little money but were rich in other ways.

Just before I turned thirteen years old I went to a little Baptist home youth club down the road from my house. The Ward family owned a beautiful home at the crest of Beacon Hill, which they used as a venue for this weekly group. It was called MYC, for Masters Youth Club, and it catered for young teenagers.

We played games, swam, sang songs and learned about the Bible. It was there that God, who lived under my bed from when I lived in Cape Town, relocated to living in my heart. However, the vagaries of different denominations passed me by and I was pretty much open to all kinds of expressions of faith.

I was a copious reader and one story that fascinated me was the story of the three children of Fatima. The Blessed Virgin Mary, the Mother of God, appeared six times to three shepherd children near the town of Fatima, Portugal between May 13 and October 13, 1917. Appearing to the children, the Blessed Virgin told them that She had been sent by God with a message for every man, woman and child living in our century, promising that Heaven would grant peace to all the world if Her requests for prayer, reparation and consecration were heard and obeyed. I never understood all She said but considering I had found God under my bed when I was three the thought of having visions and close personal encounters with the Divine was thrilling. I bought a Rosary and tried my best to get better acquainted with Mother Mary.

Nun-hood beckoned. My heart was set on becoming Sister Pamela the Prayerful and I would bring help and healing to a hurting world. However, it brought tears to my mother's eyes as the notion of having no grandchildren was too much to bear. It brought a smile to my dad's face as his future financial demands towards me would be minimal.

My burgeoning Catholic bent wasn't sustained in the long term however, as I had a Catholic friend at school, Vivien, who put the fear of God into me. She stated with great authority that if I miss Mass even once, I would go to Hell. Heck, I didn't even GO to Mass! I went to Hillside Methodist Church at the time. I was doomed. I gave up Catholicism and stuck to the Methodists and later, to the Baptist church where all the good looking boys went.

In those days entertainment was not digital nor was it instant. Internet wasn't even a twinkle in the eye of Tim Berners-Lee's, inventor of the World Wide Web. The only tablet we had was called aspirin. Phone calls to friends had a strict time limit and our parents had to drive us to every social appointment. So we did a whole lot of home entertainment.

Dress code for parties was long dresses for girls and smart, long-sleeved shirts and ties for boys. Fruit punch, made with a base of brewed tea, was served in a gigantic punch bowl and a hot and cold buffet was laid out in the dining room. We danced in heels on parquet flooring to thumping 70's hits, pretending we were in a proper nightclub. At a certain time of the evening, after throwing shapes vigorously and stuffing ourselves with food, the lights were dimmed until you could hardly see each other. Things now got serious. It was Slow Dancing Time.

This was when boys' teenage hormones raged and girls became bold in their allure. Dancing became the shuffle. We shuffled with our partners, belly to belly, face to face, arms wrapped around necks, sweating from such close contact in the evening heat. Couples 'got off' with each other as they shuffled in the dark, experimenting with kissing techniques as they kept one eye on other couples, hoping to pick up some tips.

My love life started perking up in Bulawayo. Tennyson Primary School held a Leavers Party for those who were moving onto high school. Boys could ask girls to be their partner. The only boy who asked me was a short Greek boy called Polydorous Polydorou. Unsurprisingly, he was called Poly for short. He was the only kid in class who had facial hair. I was made up.

My first sweetheart was Arthur, twelve years old, with a mop of curly black hair. His seduction technique consisted solely of pushing me into the public swimming pool. I screamed every time then went back for more. Sadly, at this time I was becoming conscious of my hair, which frizzed even more alarmingly after swimming, so I gave up Arthur in favour of the well-being of my hair.

I moved swiftly on to Keith. Youth groups in the 70's were the Tinder of the day and he was my swipe-right Methodist. He was also an older man, being seventeen to my thirteen. I reckon he was my first proper boyfriend. The youth group had arranged a shop-window-treasure-hunt-at-night (the fun never stopped in Bulawayo) and we were walking together in search of clues. Turning to me he growled (this was my first boyfriend whose voice had broken) 'Could I hold my girlfriend's hand?' I wondered who the hell his girlfriend was and why hadn't he told me about her. It took me a while to realise he was talking about me. I emitted a squeaky 'Yes!' and he took my hand and our fingers linked. He kissed me at the end of the evening – open-mouthed but no tongues, which would have grossed me out completely. Oh, the joy of being a woman.

I spent a lot of time with lanky Philip after Keith and I parted ways. Philip was a pale, skinny, bean-pole of a boy with a shock of blue-black hair sweeping over his forehead. He had a very noble nose, just large and hooked enough to appear aristocratic. He was the one who taught me that a ridiculous sense of humour and laughter was the way forward in matters of the heart.

My education regarding love escalated exponentially with the arrival of Sally.

My parents decided they would become foster parents. Actually I am jolly sure it was entirely my mother's idea and my dad just agreed to it. I have a feeling his acquiescence had something to do with his philandering and the resultant power play between him and my mother. So Sally arrived to stay for a short while.

Sally was sixteen and already a woman of the world, which is probably why she was in the fostering progamme to begin with. She was a wild child with strawberry-blonde hair, freckles and the body of Marilyn Monroe. I snuck into her room one day to look through her drawers and hit the jackpot. There, in her bedside table drawer, were Peter Styvesant cigarettes and a box of matches. Sally smoked! This was the most awful piece of knowledge to possess. As a former wanna-be nun I was deeply shocked.

This was not the worst of Sally's sins however. That had to be when she taught me how to French kiss and do the most stupendous love bites.

She was a true teacher and led by example. Holding her arm up to her mouth she demonstrated, with slurpy sound effects, just how to kiss a bloke using tongues, which from what I saw, involved plenty of spit as well. I had to copy her using my own arm as a boyfriend. There was far too much sweat and saliva for my liking but I closed my eyes and French kissed the hairs right off my salty skin.

The art of love-biting followed, which was a form of French kissing that included the use of teeth and the gift of suck. A good love-bite left a purple-blue bruise the size of a coin, strategically placed so that it would be visible to one's peers. I sported a few good bruises on my forearm for some weeks before I got the chance to actually do one on another human's neck.

Part of the youth club scene in Bulawayo was connected to the imposing Catholic Church on the edge of town. Christ the King Church was also called the Lemon Squeezer due to its fruity architectural design. It wasn't the only fruity thing going on though, as discos for teenagers took place there on a Friday night.

Flashing lights, ear-splitting music, orange cordial and an assortment of randy teenagers made for an exciting night out. It was like speed-dating on a turntable next to revolving doors. Kids got off with each other, pledging allegiance for at least an hour and a half before spotting a new, better-looking conquest across the strobe-lit room. I reckon Christ the King was not amused but at least it got kids to church.

* * *

My family life was interesting at this point. My mother was beautiful, curvaceous, bubbly and sociable. She was also depressed, spiritual and had a bloody good aim when throwing stilettos at disobedient children. She was a society hostess, married to a well-to-do man who brought home the bacon. He also brought home evidence of other beautiful woman and my mother could decipher this like the best CSI detective in the world.

Shouting down the phone at the other woman of the moment was particularly interesting. I could not believe my mother had such inventive vocabulary.

My father's personal revolving female turntable was linked to his business success as well as to his extremely handsome appearance. He had a fantastic singing voice, played sport and told jokes like a born comedian. He was The Man! The local ladies flocked to him and he loved every minute of it. My mother did not.

A side-effect of all this adulation at this time was my father's love for a good social life which included a vast consumption of alcohol. One night he arrived home late, nicely pickled, to an irate wife. My mother was in bed when he arrived but he dragged her out onto the parquet floor of the hall. The commotion woke me up and I crept out of my bed down the passage towards the lounge. I saw my father dragging my mother along the floor by her heels. She was dressed in her shortie nightie, which ruched behind her as she was pulled along, exposing her naked body. My father bellowed drunkenly as he pulled her, yanking her down the couple of steps that led to our lounge. It was then my mother saw me peeking out behind the passage wall. She waved at me, saying I should not worry, it's all okay and I should go back to bed. I didn't believe it for a second but I shot to my room, climbed under my blankets and pulled the pillow over my head. It's a memory that still haunts me today.

My mother's dressing table was a shrine to beauty. She owned countless bottles of perfume, beautiful hairbrushes and trays of make-up. She also had a head made of Styrofoam which held her current wig. I found this a little creepy. Charlie was her favourite perfume for a while and when her much-loved cousin, Uncle Norman, came to talk to her whilst she was at her dressing table, she squirted this liberally in the air and trilled, 'Come smell my Charlie!' They both giggled like kids.

My mother was a hands-on mother. She considered a slap or a hiding as part of good parenting. As mentioned before, her shoe-throwing was legendary. She also had a rest routine in the afternoons where she called all four of her children to her double bed. We each had a 'spot'. The worst spot for me was curled up, facing her face. I breathed her breath. It was nasty. Although the other spot that was especially daunting was the space between her rear end and her calves. This was danger on an altogether different level. Passing wind in a high-decibel manner was her gift. She could even play tunes. Once we had slept for an hour like a litter of kittens we could stretch, extricate ourselves from a tangle of sweaty limbs and get up.

Her hands-on parenting style extended to giving us worm medicine every few months, malt every night and an enema once a week. Some memories are difficult to erase. If only I'd known that colonic irrigation would become a 'thing' in the future and people would pay for it to be done. I've missed out on a massive career opportunity.

The Bulawayo newspaper published an article about my mother. She had seen a UFO from our balcony in the midnight sky. It had hovered just beyond the house and some sort of messages were relayed. She was a mini-celebrity. My father was mortified and I just thought she was barmy. Shortly after that she was taken to hospital by ambulance. I never knew if these two events were linked.

My mother's annual Grape Diet was greatly feared by all who lived with her. The Grape Diet wasn't rocket science – one just had to eat grapes for thirty days and nothing else. Apparently this cleansed your innards and the pounds fell off like spilled wine. Her grape box arrived every few days and she clutched at it like a mad woman. If one of us went near the box to pinch a grape she yelled through gritted teeth, 'STEP AWAY FROM THE GRAPES! THEY'RE MINE! Her moods became very fluid, flowing from crazed to super-duper mental in the blink of an eye. We slunk silently around the house, squirreling food in our rooms so she wouldn't see something edible that did not resemble a grape. I never knew if her insides were cleansed but I did know that my nerves were completely shot for one month of the year.

My brother David was my tormentor. He teased me mercilessly and in return I whined to my mother and 'told on him', which didn't really do anything to solve the issue. I must admit, I was quite annoying. David is responsible for my two scars on my left leg. I got the first one when we were riding to school on our bicycles and he rode straight into me as we were racing each other. We went down in a tangle of spokes and pedals and handlebars, one of which caught me below the knee and ripped my flesh wide open, like a great big bloody smile. Six stitches later I hobbled out of hospital and played the 'poor me' card for quite some time. The second injury came when we were playing around a rusty old washing line pole. David swung a piece of jagged metal my way and it caught me on top of my knee, gouging out a very deep triangular chunk of flesh. We have always had a tempestuous relationship.

Discipline in our family home was old-school. My mother's usual response, apart from shoe-throwing, was yelling, 'just wait until your father gets home!' So when he did get home he had the job of giving us a hiding. There were times when he'd have to give all of us a hiding and we had to wait in our bedrooms for our punishment to be administered. My parents usually were polite enough to ask, 'Do you want a hiding?' when we were getting out of hand. They did not seem to understand that actually, no, I'd prefer not to be given a hiding, if it's all the same to you.

At group hidings time, my dad started at one end of the house, with Peter's room, then moved to Jenny's, then David's, then mine, which was the last room at the end of the passage. He took his belt off and gave us each a whipping. Hearing the shrieks and the yelps from my siblings as he moved along the passage way was scarier than the actual hiding. Very occasionally, when he was feeling generous, he told us to scream as he whipped the bedding to make my mother think we'd been suitably chastised.

One of the things most of us kids had genetically inherited was a blinding set of buck teeth. This came from my mother's side. Crissy hair and wide, child-bearing hips also came as part of our genetic richness. My Aunty Patsy's hair was so wiry she could have been used as a pot scourer and my other aunties on my father's side were so extremely broad in the beam it was easier for them to enter a room sideways.

My dad took David to Johannesburg a few times a year to see the orthodontist. He had the benefit of having his buck teeth seen to as he was the oldest, so he sported a brace long before it was considered cool. As the second child, my sticky-out gnashers were left alone, with the unfulfilled hope I would grow into them. Peter's teeth were not so buck, as overly generous, and he managed to grow into his with minimal help. The buck-tooth fairy by-passed Jenny entirely.

Going 'down South' was a wondrous thing. South Africa was a land of delicious chocolates, fish paste, Bovril and Milo. My father came home laden with goodies after every trip and my mother squirreled these away and eked them out over the next few months.

My social life and my spiritual life were closely entwined. In Bulawayo you could go the sporting route, the nightclub route or the church route. I was too chubby for the sporting pathway, too meek and timid for the nightclub shenanigans and just right for the church highway.

Faith and friends went together. There was lots of guitar-playing, chorus-singing and flared, orange trousers. We praised the Lord whilst wearing Jesus sandals or towering platform shoes. I spent many nights at Christian camps in the Matopos hills surrounding Bulawayo, feeling like I was touching heaven and hearing the whisper of God's voice over the boulders. We'd get there by piling into the open backs of lorries and hurtle down dirt roads towards camp. I loved the magic of the dawn, hearing the wild birds chatter and seeing the sun rise above the rocks. I felt profoundly close to God in those ancient hills.

* * *

In 1975 my father got a new job 'down South' and Johannesburg became our new home.

However, I stayed in Bulawayo to finish my term at Townsend Girls High School.

I lived with a friend of mine from school for this time. She was Jewish and her family had a home in Kumalo, the very wealthy Jewish area of Bulawayo. So this added beautifully to my experience in Spiritualism, Catholicism, Methodism and the Baptists; I was soon Shabbating and Shalomming with the best of them. I loved the Jewish food and I loved my friend, Linda. I hated the three Chihuahuas that ruled the house. They barked at me from the moment they smelled me at the bottom of the driveway. They curled their thin little lips over their protruding razor teeth and made killing noises in their throats. They attacked my ankles, shrieking as if they'd caught juicy prey and they tried to bring me down. This everyday occurrence encouraged both my prayer life and my imagination, as I simultaneously prayed for protection and thought of how many possible ways there were by which I could annihilate the little buggers.

It was at Townsend where I learned to do Scottish dancing. We did this in our PE lessons. Quite how relevant Scottish dancing was in a small town in the bowels of Africa is still not clear but it beat doing actual gym. My best friends, Morna, Wendy, Barbara and I flung ourselves enthusiastically into the Highland Fling even though not one of us possessed a dancing gene in our bodies.

Instructed to leap over 'horses' and shimmy up a rope, I was destined to fail. A forward roll was about my limit and at least my dignity kept intact, thanks to the non-negotiable issue of wearing a pair of robust school underpants that was essentially a huge, reinforced green girdle.

Athletics was also not my thing. I was once again put in the relay race, where all the dud runners were placed. I did the long-jump too, because that was better than flinging myself and my ever-increasing bosoms over an unreasonably high pole. I used to do the shortest long-jumps known to man, just hitting the sand about a metre in.

Along with the Scottish dancing, we had another cultural sporting event. It definitely felt Marxist in nature. The entire school had to be on the field to perform a staged movement to music for an audience. The practices alone were like torture and trying to co-ordinate hundreds of girls of all shapes and sizes was never going to work. I swear if we had uniforms that were slightly more utilitarian we would have been mistaken for a tipsy communist army.

My maths teacher is almost famous for being so bad. Mrs Harlan must have been a terrific maths whizz but she was an awful teacher. She spent her time eating bananas in class and talking to the blackboard upon which she scribbled algebra and other mysterious markings. I don't think she could see very well and as she didn't ever answer any of any questions, I don't think she heard very well either. At the end of her tenure there she was apparently gifted to Falcon College, the posh boys' school in the country. Just retribution as Falcon boys were snobs with parents richer than mine. I identified strongly with the Marxist principles we displayed in our exercise routine. Sharing is caring. Take that, Falcon!

I have to segue to my relationship with maths at this point.

I was never a genius at mathematics. My dad was a brilliant mathematician and my fundamental non-comprehension was a source of deep disappointment for him, not to mention a rocket booster for his blood pressure which reached figures I could not calculate when he tried to explain concepts to me.

When I was thirteen he hired an eighteen-year old bespectacled, spotty maths tutor called John who must have been brilliant inside his head but he kept his brilliance and his pulse well hidden. I could have put money on the fact he did not actually possess a spine as he slumped like over-cooked spaghetti over the table. I paid close attention to his nail-bitten hands as he scrawled interesting marks across the page but he did not solve any of my mathematical difficulties.

My brother David was similarly afflicted. His worst skill was memorising his times tables. My father would try and catch him out at dinner time in between forkfuls of macaroni cheese by barking, '6x6?' My brother would answer through cheesy teeth – '42!' At which point my father would choke noisily on his macaroni. My brother's sticking point was the answer to 7x8. Eventually he actually remembered the answer was 56 and peace reigned for a while. Unfortunately, during dinner the next night, my father quick-fired, 'what's 8x7?' at my brother, who was about to place a chicken's parson's nose in his mouth. His reaction was a forceful spitting out of said parson's nose across the table which hit my startled little sister on the chin. 'I don't know!' he wailed. He never did get the hang of his times tables. Despite that, he has a Doctorate today so maybe times tables are not that important in the greater scheme of things.

My terrors increased a thousand fold when I had to solve story sums at school.

A cattle train is travelling to Bulawayo at 60 miles an hour. There are 53 cows in 5 separate coaches and 16 bales of hay to share amongst them. A buck crosses the railway line causing the train to slow down to 34.5 miles an hour for 36 minutes. This causes a cow to calf, increasing the amount of cows to 54 in total. How much will the Bulawayo butcher charge for a rump steak in Zimbabwean dollars in 7 days time?

Story sums bear no relationship to the real world whatsoever, I am convinced.

Algebraic formulas were also too much for my arty brain. It was like trying to solve a mystery in Russian calligraphy. Solving $2v-3p=y$ held no excitement for me. If any mathematical mystery insisted on being that obtuse, it deserved to remain a mystery.

Drama was another matter. I loved this subject and I thought I was jolly good. My crowning achievements were two roles and were based on looks alone – one, a psychotic German nurse who killed her patients and the other, a main part in How the Elephant Got Its Nose. Apparently I looked naturally mean and dangerous for the nurse role. For the other, the drama teacher made me the baboon and brushed my wild and woolly hair out until it bushed crazily. I looked like I'd been electrocuted. Apparently I also have a naturally monkey face and a good coat of bodily fur too.

My dramatic forays included a stint in the annual Bulawayo Pantomime. My friend Gaynor and I decided we would do this together so I moved in with her whilst the shows were being rehearsed and performed. We were both a bit on the chunky side so decided to go on a diet of boiled eggs and water for a couple of weeks. No-one wanted to stand down-wind of us at rehearsals and we lost weight and friends in equal measure. The diet caused a boil to erupt right on the tip of Gaynor's nose and it took us ages to try to camouflage her Mt Vesuvius before every show. I so envied the lead actress; sixteen years old, with beautiful, long red hair, dainty as a fairy, daring as a fashion icon, who wore pink to enhance her hair. To top it all, she sang like a nightingale. I cavorted around in the chorus with my erupting friend and dreamed of Hollywood.

I cherish the memories I have of Gaynor. After school she became a mission worker, married and moved with her little family to the Matopos area, where we used to have our camps. There she served the local community until the on-going political uprisings generated a spate of killings. She and her family were brutally killed.

Johannesburg

My dad bought a house in Waterloo Road, Douglasdale, Sandton. It was a rambling face-brick flat-roofed house, very modern for its time and was situated at the far edge of Sandton suburbs. The grounds were half an acre in area and overlooked undeveloped countryside for the first few years of our stay. Our street was dirt, with a tree slap bang in the middle of the road near our gate. Opposite us was Douglasdale Dairy which housed cows and pigs and other farmyard animals.

The rural setting didn't last too long. A major concrete highway was built half a mile away from our house. To deal with the noise we had to pretend that it was the sea we were hearing. I had carved hearts and my beloved's name into the tree in the road and that was chopped down when our road was tarred. Just before the dairy changed into a milk depot only, one of their pigs came visiting. She trotted through our open gate and made herself at home in our garden. Unfortunately for her, our giant furry Keeshond, Fritz, took a fancy to her and behaved most outrageously. The pig was not impressed and she threw him off and ran hell for leather for the safety of the dairy. Pigs are sprinters and can run at about eleven kilometres an hour. I think she broke the piggy speed limit.

I loved this house. There were four bedrooms, two and a half bathrooms, a study, a handful of reception rooms and a huge kitchen. It was a house that saw engagements and weddings, pregnancies and babies, my parents' twenty-fifth wedding anniversary, Club 7 meetings, parties, friends and family get-togethers.

It was also where some boys from the Drakensberg Boys Choir school stayed during a tour. My brother Peter had a good voice, like my dad, who burst into song at every given opportunity. Peter was accepted into the Drakensberg Boys Choir School when he was a young boy and looked most cherubic in his blue and white frilly choral gear. Our house had ceiling to floor windows and when they were clean it appeared as if the door was open. We had bumped ourselves countless times on the glass door thinking it was open so it was an easy mistake to make. Thinking the door was indeed open one of Peter's little friends decided to run outside at full tilt and ran straight through the plate glass onto the outdoor verandah. He was so lucky he survived without being badly hurt. Thereafter, my mother stuck window stickers onto the glass which helped avoid further near death experiences. She should have learned that lesson years ago when we lived in Johannesburg for the first time, after my father dived straight through the lounge glass doors to save my brother, who was being mauled by a neighbour's dog.

One of the rooms in our house was used for many different purposes over the years. It was the spare room, an office, a sewing room, a library and a machine knitting room. Machine knitting was one of my mother's fads and we all suffered greatly from her love for this art form. The knitting machine looked like a gigantic medieval type writer. It sounded like an entire knitting factory and could even be set to keep on knitting even when the knitter was not there. Great big balls and cones of yarn were stacked onto the adjoining tables and into cupboards. Like Joseph's coat of many colours (and I quote), they were:

...red and yellow and green and brown

And scarlet and black and ochre and peach

And ruby and olive and violet and fawn

And lilac and gold and chocolate and mauve

And cream and crimson and silver and rose

And azure and lemon and russet and grey

And purple and white and pink and orange

And red and yellow and green and brown and

Scarlet and black and ochre and peach

And ruby and olive and violet and fawn

And lilac and gold and chocolate and mauve

And cream and crimson and silver and rose

And azure and lemon and russet and grey

And purple and white and pink and orange

And blue.

The colour combinations chosen by my mother for her creations were truly atrocious. Mustard, olive green and brown were amongst her favourite colours. One of the easiest patterns to knit on the machine was stripes so we were blessed with many a stripy jumper to wear. We were grateful that Johannesburg had a very brief winter season. The knitting machine eventually broke down but nobody admitted anything.

One night my mother saved us from burglars. She heard a noise in the middle of the night and decided to investigate. If there is one thing you do not do in South Africa, is to investigate a midnight sound by yourself. Burglars carried weapons and householders were likely to be trussed up, shot at or beaten if they confronted them. Instead, my mother rose from her bed, stark naked, and proceeded to tiptoe down the passage to the lounge, a fair distance in this ranch-style house. She passed the knitting room and our bedrooms, took a quick look around the darkened lounge and tiptoed back to bed, satisfied all was ticketty-boo.

In the morning we awoke to the sight of our lounge glass doors broken and evidence of items being stolen. We then worked out that my mother, naked as a baby, had passed the burglars who had hidden in the knitting room. The sight of my mother in all her glory was clearly enough to make the burglars scarper. Or maybe they had seen some of her stripy jumpers as they were hiding in the room and got out before she made one for them.

Starting school in my penultimate high school year at Bryanston High School in Sandton, part of greater Johannesburg, was a revelation. Coming from an all-girls, British-style school into a high school that had actual boys attending was very scary. They were noisy and rude. They swaggered. They smelled ripe. They had acne. I was not a happy bunny.

I managed to collect a cohort of friends. Each one was already on the margins of school society so we felt we belonged together. We were too tall, too short, too clever, too fat or too plain to be part of the 'in' group so we formed our own. We ruled the quadrangle step. We changed the world. We bought tuck even though most of us were fat. We tutted over girls who put Vaseline on their eyelashes to look as if they wore mascara. We never smoked in the toilets. We did our homework.

My first special friend at Bryanston High School was Judy. She came from a large family of Christian Scientists and we spent lots of our time talking about faith. Judy had started embracing born-again Christianity, fusing it with layers of Christian Scientist beliefs. She was a rebel on both sides of the faith argument. One Christmas I was asked to join her and her family in their holiday house on the South Coast. It was my first Christmas away from my family so I was a little apprehensive.

My apprehension was replaced by warm feelings of contentment as well as by inappropriate giggles when they hosted their Christmas party and I drank a couple of glasses of wine. Judy's older brother, who was twenty-four, was called Guy. He was dead handsome, with slanty eyes and straight jet-black hair that stuck out ever so sexily. Although he was completely out of my league I had a crush on him and tried to act really grown up by tossing back alcohol. All I got for my efforts was some help in getting to bed and a mega-headache in the morning.

Judy and I both wanted to be baptized. We had learned all about what it meant at our youth group and were committed to fulfilling the call. So we took ourselves off into the sea shallows on one beautiful summer's day and baptized each other. In turn, we knelt in the gentle, foaming surf and allowed the other to do the dunking as we committed our lives to God through baptism. It was highly unorthodox but I took it very seriously.

One of my friends was absolutely beautiful. Too beautiful for the 'in' crowd so we welcomed her in to our motley crew. Her name was Sue and she had glorious straight black hair that flowed down her back like an ebony waterfall. Sue and I lived near each other. We had to cross a triangular piece of veld and by-pass a pond when we visited. My parents were fine with that until the 16th June, 1976. They forbade me to walk alone because there had been an uprising and white people were in danger. I heard the news on television but didn't understand the reasons why it occurred or the scale of violence involved. It left me with uneasy questions but my teenage self-centredness pushed these kinds of issues to the back of my mind.

16 June, Tens of thousands of high school students took to the streets to protest against compulsory use of Afrikaans at schools. Police opened fire on marching students, killing thirteen-year old Hector Petersen and at least three others. This begins what becomes known as the Soweto youth uprising. The student uprising spread to other parts of the country leaving over 1,000 dead, most of whom being killed by the police.

Sue actually had a life outside school, unlike the rest of us and she introduced me to a group of kids that would impact my life forever.

Club 7 was a youth group started at Rouxville Baptist Church in Johannesburg, opposite the Doll's House, a famous drive-in restaurant and oh, so trendy in the 70s and 80s.

At the height of Club 7 days, a hundred kids gathered for mid-week prayer meetings, Friday night Club 7 meetings, camps and outings. They were joyous occasions. We wanted to transform the world and get to know Jesus evermore personally. Teenagers came from all over Johannesburg. The North, where Sue and I lived, was the rich and spoiled part of the compass, the South was considered poor and rough, the East was conservative and kids from there had very bad accents and the West was a mystery, a bit dodgy but no-one could quite decide why.

Having come from Bulawayo not too long before, I was astounded at the difference in the residential areas. I had been so protected and surrounded by good old Colonial wealth I hardly knew how to process it all. When I went for a Club travelling dinner in the South, the main course was macaroni and mince. Mince! I felt so sorry for the Southerners and for the other members who lived in any area that was not the North. I was a Colonial through and through.

A few kind older kids did the collecting and dropping off home. We were bussed in, crammed into station wagons, Kombis, Volkswagen Beetles and other modes of transport that defied description and ran on prayer and no gas.

Although we were connected to Rouxville Baptist Church many members and leaders found us annoying and rebellious. They were quite right. At times it must have seemed to them they were overrun with hormonal beatniks who sang choruses to the most Holy God whilst lifting their hands or clapping. IN CHURCH. It's a good thing they never saw what we got up to outside of church.

We were very earnest in our desire to change the world and to follow the Bible's teachings. It was sometimes a bit like the blind leading the blind but our passion could not be faulted. At one point we discovered, by some random authority, that a woman had to have her head covered in church. The blokes had to remove their hats. Go figure. At any rate, the Club 7 girls started to wear mantillas as a sign of submission and respect during church services. No such respect was demanded at youth group meetings thankfully. So lacy, beautiful mantillas were tucked into our handbags, withdrawn and draped across our hair at the appropriate time. I felt very holy. This fad didn't last too long, thank the good Lord, and the mantilla-wearing quietly made a discreet exit after a while.

Club 7 chose leaders to lead the group. It was all very democratic; we submitted our candidates who then presented their views, then we all went away to pray, came back to vote and the elected leader was chosen. Unfortunately democracy did not include girls or ugly boys who didn't play guitar and sing.

Leaders influenced the group a great deal. Doug was strong, principled and a born preacher. He encouraged us to avoid listening to the radio or play secular music or watch television that would turn our focus away from our spiritual path. I did all that then later discovered with horror that Doug had a radio in his car and he listened to it all the time! He said he wanted to keep up with the news. I stored that little nugget of subterfuge in my head and got on with loving everyone with the love of the Lord.

Our passion for the Lord also extended to passion for the opposite sex. Hormones raged. Hanky-panky occurred followed by swift repentance and the promise never to go so far again. Couples formed and split apart. One young leader, with almost zero sexual experience, gave us a talk all about sex and how to overcome urges without masturbating, which he declared was a wicked act. We all nodded wisely and got on with our sinful lives anyway.

Homosexuality was definitely a big sin. One beautiful boy, Jay, was our token gay and he took the eye of a leader and a few other Club members, including girls. The gay was not prayed out of him despite the best efforts of his Club 7 friends. Being gay was even worse than masturbating.

Sue and one of our leaders, Kevin, had a bit of a romance going in the early days. She was an exotic goddess and he was beautifully built and handsome as a movie star. They were the Posh and Becks of their time. I fancied Kevin too after they broke up. I fancied him for one week then moved on to Steve.

Steve said he'd first realised he liked me when he saw me praying passionately under a tree in the church grounds one hot day. It may have been the day a hornet was trying to attack me and I was beseeching God to save me or it may have been just me, being godly. I'll go with the godly.

He was sweet and kind and polite. Steve was a leader at one time for the group; he had a gentle spirit and beautiful eyelashes. Of course, he could play the guitar and sing. He had floppy dark hair that he flicked to the side and a bright orange Beetle. He lived in an area called Orange Grove, near the Club 7 headquarters with his mum and his sister. Although still working through my issues of believing others were grossly deprived, I loved the bohemianism of his home. His mum was a divorced working single mum, unusual in those days, and his house had a verandah facing the road. The neighbours were within spitting distance. There was no garden laid to lawn surrounding a swimming pool. There was a grassy patch at the back where Steve played with his beautiful, golden dog. I loved his sister too and she became my bridesmaid when I married another. There was just so much love in the house.

Our relationship had an innocence about it. We learned what it was to love and laugh and enjoy a wonderful social life. We learned the language of love through touch and kissing and just about managed to stay within the Christian bounds of 'not going too far'. We coped with that because actually there was no place to go and get jiggy –the lack of venue was our saving grace. The thing about being in love at the start of adulthood is that inevitably, it all ends.

After I returned from my three-month travels, things were different. I was different. I was exposed to all sorts of visuals, experiences, debates and ways of life that radically opened my mind. Steve had stayed and done some growing of his own. At first we were so happy to back together and he spoke about getting married and what the future may look like. Seemed as if it was the very next week when he took me on a date to the planetarium to look at the heavens. I thought this was very romantic and had stars in my eyes and hope in my heart. He was distant though and at the end of the show he sat me down and declared the relationship was over.

I felt like a Mills and Boon heroine. Heartbroken, I faced the future with a steady resolve. My dark, brooding stranger-lover was out there somewhere, just waiting to be found. As it turned out, he was closer than I thought.

* * *

After school graduation I worked at the local post office for a few months. This was not a thing that Bryanston kids did. We were considered university material and too posh for postal positions but I had decided to take a gap year, work a bit and travel. Working there opened my eyes to how the other half lived.

The post office was run by a short, round, hairy Afrikaans man with issues. Meneer Oosthuizen looked like Obelix on a bad day and smelled like a tobacco factory. His bushy moustache was yellow from smoking and his teeth were tawny beige. He spat when he talked and was aggressive as hell. He was eye-level with my bosom and loved pressing against me as he showed me how to do things, like tear off stamps from the stamp sheet. He showed me how to wield the rubber stamp by standing behind me and rubbing himself up against me, holding my hand in his as he demonstrated this supremely difficult task.

A giant of a black man worked at the post office, doing all the menial jobs. His name was Piet and he had a smile that lit up the world. Meneer Oosthuizen, who came up to Piet's waist, hated Piet and punished him for mistakes by kicking him down to the floor and screaming in his face. He was brutal. These were apartheid days and Piet didn't have the wherewithal to complain. I didn't have a clue what to do to make it stop.

The Bryanston post office, like all services and shops, was divided into two sections, a white and a non-white section. I was given the cramped, non-white section to service and soon realised that there was more to my world than I thought. People queued up patiently to transfer their wages to family back home in the Tribal Trust Lands and send letters to their children who they saw once or twice a year. Some needed help to write addresses. There was a sense of camaraderie in this little section and a great deal of laughter. I learned more than stamp-tearing from my customers. I mainly learned how little I knew about people from whom I was separated by law and by custom.

From Fuengirola to Fez

After this work experience I went overseas for three months. It was 1977 and Sue and I were going to travel to Canada, The United Kingdom and Europe. Unexpectedly Sue had to cancel her trip so I adjusted my plans and flew off all by myself to London.

Now, bearing in mind that at eighteen years old, I had never caught a bus, or booked a taxi, or flown overseas or indeed, shouldered any grown-up responsibilities at all, this was an adventure of note.

It was before the days of mobile phones, faxes and iPads. We had dial-face phones with handles at home and overseas I had to find a red phone booth in London and a special phone centre for overseas calls whilst in other places. I was alone, with a suitcase as heavy as sin and a naivety that was alarming. My first task was to get off the plane at Heathrow, find a taxi and go to a hotel that my dad had booked for me for the first week.

The hotel was not what I was expecting. I came from Africa, where the hotels we had always stayed in had suites adorned in matching soft furnishings, an en-suite bathroom with shiny tiled floors and walls and a view. Men dressed in uniforms would take our bags from the car to the room and we'd sit in the lounge with a drink, listening to piped music before heading into the exciting outdoors.

Well, this place was a skinny building of three floors, super-glued between other skinny buildings with the front door right on the road. Cars honked, people scurried past, cyclists tried to survive the chaos and nobody looked me in the eye. I heaved my case out of the taxi boot, paid what seemed like half my trip budget to the driver, and entered a new world.

After checking in at a hole in the entrance wall which was the office I dragged my bags upstairs to the third floor. The passage and stair ways were dark, the carpets a swirl of lurid colours cleverly covering up the vomit I could smell in the dusty air. My bedroom had a bed on a wire frame, wallpaper that someone had obviously created after an acid trip and a basin. The bathroom was a shared facility down the passage. I cried.

The next morning a very fair-haired English girl entered my room to make up the bed. I nearly passed out. She was the housemaid? I had to take a moment to think this through. I had never, in all my years, had a white cleaner do my room. In Rhodesia we had house boys, young black men who lived with the family and learned the crafts of house-keeping, cooking, driving and gardening. When I was growing up in Bulawayo we had a little silver bell on our dining table that we'd ring to let the house boy know it was time to clear the table or time for the next course. My shoes were polished and my clothes set out for me for the day. My bed was made every day by a house boy. This lifestyle continued in Johannesburg where black women were the housekeepers and maids. Taking one more glance at this pale cleaner I shot out my room to let her get on with it without me looking at her with an open mouth and bush baby eyes.

And so my overseas adventure began and the travel bug took up residence in my soul.

I explored London, taking numerous photographs that I had to develop back at home. My budget was very limited so I took the all-inclusive famous Full English Breakfast for all it had. I ate like a starving person, hoovering in baked beans, bacon, sausage, eggs, tinned tomatoes and toast like an award-winning Electrolux. Then I packed my pockets with spare toast and wrapped-up butters and any fruit that caught my eye. Stuffed, I sauntered out the entrance to start my day of sight-seeing. At the end of the day I bought an ice-cream and this eating plan saw me through.

Sights and sounds I had never experienced before accosted my senses; red buses, ancient architecture, avenues lined with old oaks in green parks, nationalities of all the world running like lemmings through tube tunnels, naughty magazines at eye level in corner city shops. Black people and white people openly holding hands in the streets, showing love across the colour divide. Newspapers with stories about a South Africa I didn't recognise. Television programmes on late at night in the communal hotel lounge that showed bare breasts and what the British called 'romping'.

I took up smoking. It was the least I could do.

I became brave and caught the ferry to Amsterdam, then travelled through Germany, staying in Dusseldorf and The Black Forest. From there I went to join a friend, Cathy, who was holidaying with her Swiss family in Neuchatel, Switzerland. We caught cable cars to the top of the Alps and drank in the snowy majesty. We lunched by the lake in Geneva and spent time at the Matterhorn, awestruck by its crooked beauty.

After a further time of sight-seeing in London and Manchester, I joined up with a Travel Camping Tour company called Transit for 18-30 year olds. I had never camped before other than going on a caravanning holiday with my parents when we were little and we'd taken our maid with us to help. It wasn't easy. I couldn't even wield a mallet successfully so was a liability for my fellow travellers from the very beginning.

We travelled by coach to France and spent our first night in Paris. I had heard about the romance of Paris but didn't expect to fall in love with it. On a night of a low-slung, heavy full moon, surrounded by gentle music and sounds of Paris, I stared at the Eiffel Tower as if I was in a dream. I wished I had someone to share it with but had to content myself by storing this romantic beauty in my heart. The romance continued as we visited Chateau after Chateau, vineyard after vineyard and with it, I discovered the joy of drinking wine.

I also discovered how little I knew about my country, South Africa. Terry was an Australian radical and waxed eloquently about our racist regime. Being young, protected and uneducated in matters of government I struggled to have a decent debate. He asked what I thought about the treatment of Steve Biko. Steve who? And what about Nelson Mandela's imprisonment? Nelson? Isn't he the terrorist who wants to kill whites? My ignorance knew no bounds. It was my second glimpse that something was not quite right in my adopted homeland.

Spain was all about food, Fuengirola and fighting. Bull fighting, that is. I had the dubious privilege of attending a bullfight with my tour group so found myself seated in an arena surrounded by a cheering crowd. The anticipation was palpable and as the first bull was released into the ring the crowd roared its approval. The bull takes a long time to die. It's teased at first and speared a number of times before the matador comes out to finish the job in style. The bleeding bull, frenzied with pain and confusion, charges blindly at the matador, who dances around it like a whirling dervish, cape in hand. When the audience's blood lust is sated, the matador shows his skill by thrusting the killing sword just at the right place to kill the bull immediately. The smell of blood soaks the senses for days to come. Bull fighting is not an uplifting experience for man or beast.

Mint tea in a Moroccan medina sounds so exotic but this marked my first claustrophobic panic attack. I wandered through the medina, or market place, in Fez, looking for bargains to buy as gifts. The lanes between stalls became increasingly narrow and dark. I was jostled relentlessly by braying animals laden with produce, vendors loudly selling their wares and chattering locals shopping for food, clothes and supplies. Personal space was not a widely practised concept in Morocco at the best of times and this was pure, crushing bedlam. My chest started hurting and I couldn't breathe. I could no longer see the sky. Waves of nausea washed over me and I stumbled down alley after alley, trying to find someone from my group to help me. I finally saw someone I knew and collapsed into their arms, drenched in sweat and heart beating at ninety to the dozen. I sat down at a rooftop cafe and was served sweet mint tea which helped bring the world back into alignment once more.

The Sahara desert in moonlight is magical. We camped at the foot of an enormous dune and settled in for the night. As darkness fell, the moon rose, full and fat, milky white. It hung suspended, low down in the night sky, dusting the tops of dunes with pale light, like a benediction. Leaving there in the morning, we drove over vast expanses of cracked desert sand, a lunar landscape as far as the eye could see.

One day we visited a camel market. Camels aren't the prettiest of creatures and their dental hygiene is atrocious. Their manners are not particularly highbrow either and they are downright grumpy. Camel rides were offered at exorbitant prices but I could not come all this way and turn down such an opportunity, despite being dressed in a halter-neck mini dress. My camel was passive-aggressive. He obediently knelt down in front of me at his handler's command, snorting and rolling back his lips to display his gnashers. I stood on a helpful little stool next to him to make it easier for me to mount the old curmudgeon. There is no graceful, ladylike way to mount a camel, especially if the mounter is dressed inappropriately. There is also no graceful, ladylike way to ride a camel in such attire. Upon heaving myself onto the saddle belly first and limbs akimbo, I grabbed the pommel and tried to assume an upright position. At this point the camel rose, creaking and bellowing its displeasure. It felt like I was riding a huge mechanical bull and all my bodily appendages were flung into all directions of the wind at the same time. As the camel criss-crossed the sandy ground my breasts bounced outrageously, with a life completely of their own and my belly rolled like the Saharan dunes. Supportive undergarments would have helped. Next time I meet a camel I'll be sure to wear my Spanx and a good old fashioned cross-your-heart bra.

Todra Gorge was starkly beautiful. A dark green valley between rocky red cliffs, it oozed mystery and just a hint of malice. We slept on the flat roof of an inn, the stars our night-light and the warm breeze our blanket. Unfortunately, besides mystery, the gorge also oozed the unmistakable odour of diarrhoea. The inn's bathroom facilities were the worst of the entire trip. It was the traditional hole with two tiles on either side for feet and a bucket next to the hole for used paper but two factors contributed to its dire state. The first factor was a dose of diarrhoea that hit all the occupants of our coach tour. The second was the fact that the loo paper was waxy, so rather than being absorbent it merrily redistributed one's yellow-brown, bubbly effluent nicely over one's lower regions. This waxy piece of delight was then placed into an overflowing bin next to one's right ear whilst one was squatting. Trying not to breathe and balance at the same time is awkward and as the foot tiles were slippery with bodily fluids, getting up from one's squat was supremely dangerous.

We celebrated the end of our Moroccan adventure by having a North African themed fancy dress party. Two fellow travellers and I opted to be a camel herder and his camel. I was the arse-end of the camel, by virtue of my voluptuous backside, apparently. I obviously did an exceedingly good job of being a camel's bottom as we won first prize.

When we returned to London, two Australian girls from the trip and I decided to hire a car to tour the West Country. They were big girls, both six feet tall. This was not taken into account when we rented the cheapest car available, a Mini. Think Mr Bean in female triplicate. Chugging down the Cornish lanes was a sight-seeing disaster as the roads were edged by walls and hedges taller than the car. We drove through a winding green tunnel for most of our time in Cornwall. We'd run out of money for our last night so ended up sleeping in the Mini outside a pub in Box. I took the driver's seat so had the steering wheel jamming me in all night whilst the two six-footers wrapped their limbs around gear sticks and head rests and tried to get some shut-eye.

I flew out of London the next day, a little homesick but vowing to return.

Marriage and Mayhem

I only went to the Johannesburg College of Education (JCE) because Steve and I were still going out and I didn't want to go too far away. Sometimes choices are made for the most ridiculous reasons yet turn out to have the best outcomes. Steve's best friend at that time was Tony, who had a girlfriend called Kathy.

Kathy and I ended up in college together and immediately became life-long buddies. When we both broke up with our boys we joined forces, thanked the good Lord for our lucky escapes and conquered our corner of the world together. We were like Little and Large. Kathy was an award-winning gymnast, short, slim and very, very bendy. I was none of those things. She also had political views and I was still pretty ignorant of political affairs. A bit like Laurel and Hardy, we worked.

Kathy and I boarded in Reith Hall for my first year at College. Residence hall living was a great start to adulthood. I could do what I wanted and still take my washing home on the weekends to be laundered. The halls were co-run by student committees and each resident was given duties to perform. I had to man the switchboard which was a huge contraption with wires that had to be attached and detached then re-attached for every call. It was like fighting a few amorous octopi and I cut off more calls than I connected.

The highlight of Fresher's week was the greatly anticipated TRAF Mooning. The boys' hall of residence was not on our campus for reasons of propriety but they had an annual tradition. The First Years, called TRAFS (FARTS cleverly spelled backwards) danced their way down the road to the girls' residences to hoot and holler and basically make a fool of themselves. The climax of their act was a group mooning. Girls lined the windows of the three eight storey towers to catch an eyeful as best they could. Binoculars helped. There was a roar of applause when the TRAFS lined up, bums to the buildings, then bent over and yanked their trousers down. White glutes glowed in the car park. Another year had begun.

My favourite subject at JCE was Blackboard. Yep, back in the day that was an actual subject. Computers were huge things that were housed in hangars and there were no such things as screens except for overhead projectors, if you were lucky enough to source one. Mrs Denham was our teacher. She was a middle-aged woman of enormous girth from her waist down. She wafted into class like a ship in full sail, her lovely face beautifully made up and her blonde hair twisted into a French roll. She taught us how to write neatly and correctly on the board, how to draw equidistant lines with the long board ruler and how to make a board clean as a whistle.

My major was Art, which I loved except for pottery and sculpture. I cannot do 3-D in any which way so trying to form a uniform shape out of clay was beyond my abilities. I have deleted all memories of trying to use the pottery wheel. One sculpture task was to create a string sculpture somewhere within the campus. So I asked Alan, who was my husband by then, to come and help me. We found a staircase outdoors and ran around it and nearby trees and bushes with balls of string until it resembled a web spun by a drunken, giant spider. I got an A for that and could never figure out why.

My best art subject was life drawing. Nude life drawing to be precise. The only adult naked bodies I had ever been exposed to in my life were those of my mum and my husband, so this was a revelation. Drawing these models gave me such an appreciation for the human form in all its dimensions and was certainly more exciting than pottery.

* * *

Club 7 was an unlicensed marriage bureau and this is where I met my first husband. Alan was a quiet, kind man who blended effortlessly in the background. He had olive skin, dark hair and deep, dark eyes. He also had a splendid bushy brown beard. His nickname was The Rabbi.

Alan was the Club taxi and he ferried everyone around Johannesburg, fetching and carrying them to and from Club events in his white station wagon. Once, Steve and I made out in the back of his wagon whilst Alan drove me home. He never complained.

We had known each other for a few years and a short while after Steve and I broke up he asked me to dinner. Alan was a bit older than most of the guys in our group so he did this properly. He avoided The Doll's House, booked a posh restaurant in town, dressed in a suit, opened the door of the car and restaurant for me and treated me like a lady. I was impressed.

We were terribly unsuited according to my parents, our friends and presumably, the rest of the world. My parents were well-off, his mum worked hard to make ends meet. He had left school the year before matriculating and worked at the airways. I achieved a good Matric result and was studying to be a teacher. He knew things about nature and could classify plants and birds expertly. I did not know the difference between a rose and a carnation. He hardly spoke. I spoke enough for the both of us. I think we complemented each other.

Growing up, my favourite story in the world was Little Women. Naturally, I was Jo, dreaming of being a writer, misunderstood and not as beautiful or as clever as anyone else. Like Jo, I had found my Professor Bhaer.

Alan had worked for South African Airways for many years but by the time we started going out, he had left to study at Rosebank Bible College. Some of our early dates were spent talking in the beautiful shady gardens of the College. His College days brought another forever friend into my life, Liz. She also studied at Rosebank and Alan introduced me to her. She lived with us for a while after we were married and her gentleness taught me so much. Like all of my closest friends, she has proved to be a strong, resilient woman who has used her intelligence and caring nature to bring about real change in her community.

Alan asked me to marry him under a lovely bridge in the veld, just south of Bryanston, where I lived. We walked down to the river, hand in hand on a sunny day, then sat me down on a rock and took off a ring he used to wear. Then he proposed. It was romantic and sweet and I said yes. It was only some time after that I realized that the bridge of beauty was a cunningly designed sewage pipe. It may have accounted for what was to come.

Our wedding day, the 8th December 1979, was a white wedding event. This was important in those days as it showed everyone that I was still a virgin. What it didn't show was that I was a virgin by the skin of my teeth. We should have taken better heed of the teaching we received.

My mother had a breakdown whilst I was getting ready in my bridal gear. This was not helpful. She sobbed and wailed that she wasn't going to come to the wedding and that my dad should take his latest squeeze instead. I had to calm her as well as try to look radiant.

After an emotional collapse of severe proportions, she ended up coming and I sailed up the aisle on my father's arm in the Randburg Baptist Church, a twenty-year-old bride, looking virtuous, my bridesmaids – my sister Jenny, college friend Kathy and Lee, Steve's sister - trailing behind in sky blue frocks, clutching pink roses.

After a reception in a marquee in the garden at home, Alan and I went off to Kyalami Ranch, a well-known hotel on the outskirts of Sandton for our first honeymoon night.

My mother had bought me a trousseau for my honeymoon. Gone were my big pants and solidly-constructed cross-your-heart bras and in their place, a flurry of lace and ribbons. My nightgown, for the auspicious occasion of losing my virginity, was a long white gown with lace neckline; a sheer white robe covered the gown and flowed onto the floor. I changed in the bathroom, desperately hoping he would not hear me using the toilet and emerged, goddess-like, a vision of angelic purity and shaking with nerves. I was comforted knowing we had taken a sex manual with us in case we came unstuck, so to speak.

No longer a virgin, I proudly set off the next day for Utopia with my husband. This was a resort in the Magaliesberg mountains near Pretoria and we had a whole A-framed chalet to ourselves for a week before settling into a flat above a fish and chip shop on Louis Botha Avenue, one of the busiest roads in Johannesburg. It was not Utopia.

The road noise was so loud we put the telephone in the cupboard. We had to stay inside the cupboard and close the door as much as possible so we could have a conversation. The flat didn't have a stove or oven so we had a hotplate to cook on. As I was used to cooking at home for six people I carried on doing so and Alan transformed from a skinny-me-links into a well-rounded individual. We decorated the flat in autumn colours, browns and oranges and highlights of avocado green. Even the egg-flipper was orange. We were so 70s it hurt.

We were also pretty poor. I was still at College and Alan did not earn very much. We often went out hunting for discarded glass bottles which we exchanged for cash. Instead of going out to movies we cuddled naked on the sofa, watching our favourite television shows. Sometimes we had mad moments – I have photos of us dressed up, he in my frilly nightie with a full face of make-up and me in his suit and tie. We got a grey kitten and called her Dusky Ruth. Her only outside space was on the roof of the fish and chip shop, lit up at night by neon signs. We had each other and our Dusky Ruth. We were happy in our noisy, cash-strapped little bubble.

* * *

In 1981, a year and a month after we married, I graduated from the Johannesburg College of Education (JCE). I taught Junior Primary children for nearly three years which made me feel quite grown-up. I loved being Mrs Bebb, mistress of my own space and imparting knowledge to eager little minds. What I realized too, was that teacher training College didn't teach squat – you only learned how to be a teacher on the ground. This happened pretty quickly when there were thirty-five pairs of eyes watching you keenly, like wild animals cornering their prey. They knew how to bring you down.

It was then that my mother had a thought. It could have been a brain aneurism but to be generous, I'll call it a creative thought. She had always been good at cooking for family, friends and for my dad's business associates. So she decided to start a catering company. My father paled at the knowledge that many, many South African Rand notes were certain to be deep-fried into fritters and consumed by a gigantic mythical mouth but he supported her anyway.

My sister and I joined her in her new venture. We were resident caterers at The Jewish Guild, a sports and recreation Club in Morningside, Johannesburg. Jenny was pregnant and on crutches at the time, so she was tasked to sit down and make fruit salads by the bucket load. A hot, greasy kitchen was not the place for crutch-walking expectant mothers. This did not deter my mother however and she roped in a friend's very young teenage daughter who was also pregnant and the size of a house. We did not have a particularly corporate image.

One of our main duties was making and serving teas for the bowlers every Saturday and Sunday morning and afternoon. Lawn bowlers are a sub-species all by themselves. My mother and father were both competition-winning bowlers and like the bowlers at the Guild, they took the game extremely seriously. Dressed in their whites, The Guild bowlers arrived in their BMWs, Mercedes' and Jaguars ready for a day of sport. They started the day off with tea or coffee and a selection of biscuits and pastries before toddling off to their respective greens. This was not a nippy undertaking as they were aged between fifty-five and ninety and carried their heavy bowls bags with them. The sun beat down mercilessly as knees creaked, backs snapped and hips contorted, in herculean efforts to get a big black bowl to kiss a little white kitty. End after end, game after game. In. Slow. Motion.

Tea-time was the highlight of the day. We made fresh scones, gingerbread, cinnamon buns, sandwiches, chocolate cakes and mini-pizzas. Eating the tea-time treats used more calories than playing a game of bowls. Fortified, the bowlers sauntered off to play the second half of the game, before coming off for a buffet lunch at noon. Tummies heavier than bowls bags, they rolled back on the greens until afternoon tea-time was called. More ends followed, the final curved ball coming at dusk after which the bowlers gathered in the bar lounge for a plate of hot chips and a nice cold beer.

We also catered for the Rotary Club, who met at the Guild every Monday evening. They demanded three robust courses and a selection of wines and spirits, which they quickly devoured as they thought up noble ways in which they could help the starving poor.

Alongside the Guild, we also catered for Montagu Country Club, a less salubrious club than the Guild that also catered for bowlers. We were chefs ahead of our time, making dishes such as Chicken-a-la-King, beef olives and beef stroganoff for lunches.

My aunty Trudy, still as bohemian and fabulously arty-farty as ever, had a new design business, that of creating fashionable clothes for the larger lady. My mum and Aunty Trudy put a fashion show together at the club one night to show off her designs. We needed models and thankfully, most of our family had 'big bones', colossal breasts, chunky thighs and generously blobby tummies. And that was just the boys. Girls in the family were Rubenesque, curvy, sexy and luscious. We were undeniably fat. We wobbled down the gangplank, I mean the runway, with heads held high and thighs rubbing together like sandpaper in the heat. Aunty Trudy's designs were bright, bold, floaty and original and we sashayed our inner Twiggy with all we had. Naturally, given the target market, we followed this with a slap-up meal to congratulate the models and the designer.

Catering for parties and weddings was fun, apart from times when we were tidying up at the City Hall at three in the morning. Our worst experience was catering for a small wedding in one of Johannesburg's wealthiest, oldest suburbs. The bridal couple was over sixty and they lived with the groom's mother, a wizened little lady of nearly ninety who still believed it was 1950. The first problem was accepting the old dear's wedding feast contribution – a marvellous pork pie of epic proportions. Unfortunately, the pork pie was green. The sell-by date was ten *years* prior to these nuptials and the pie practically walked to the table by itself. We managed to set it proudly on the table whilst she watched then whipped it away as soon as she had scurried off. Thankfully her Alzheimer's ensured she didn't remember giving it to us in the first place.

There was a second problem however. We laid out the reception feast on a massive solid wood table in one of the reception rooms, happy that we were ahead of time. Returning as the wedding ceremony was closing, we discovered to our absolute horror, that an army of ants covered the entire table. There were ants squishing into devilled eggs, coating the salads, swimming in dressings and joyfully burying themselves in cake icing. The wedding cake was an ant mountain. We launched into a killing spree like women possessed.

My mother then decided that kind of excitement was all too much so she came up with a twisted tangent to our catering company. Koeksusters. A koeksuster is a South African invention, a twisted doughnut deep-fried in oil then dunked in sugary lemon syrup. They are extremely bad for one's health and deadly to diabetics. They pack a gazillion calories per bite and can rot the enamel off your teeth in a flash. They are delicious.

Our new mission was to make koeksusters (pronounced cook-sisters) and sell them. This was a good idea as many people were prepared to spend their money on wicked deliciousness. It turned out that it was too much of a good idea. Within a few weeks we were making then delivering eight garbage bags full of packs containing eight koeksusters each, to businesses in Johannesburg on a daily basis.

We started plaiting and twisting dough made the day before at three in the morning. Our bodies slumped at the table, exhausted, as we worked in gummy-eyed silence until all the dough was done. We made the syrup the day before too; huge pots of boiling sugar and water flavoured by slices of lemon were left to cool then plonked in the fridge to cool overnight. Once each koeksuster had been deep-fried in a big vat of oil it was plunged into the icy syrup until it had absorbed all it could. They were then set out to drain, be packaged, packed, labelled and transported. My mother drove the Kombi and I hauled orders to waiting customers.

We then returned to the kitchen to start knocking up dough and syrup for the next day. It became a prison sentence and it came to a sticky end when a food chain wanted us to provide millions of the things for their nation-wide shops. Koeksusters had lost their charm, we had lost our joie de vivre and we ran for the koeksuster-free hills. Our catering days were over.

* * *

Alan and I started trying for children within the first year of our marriage. Trying was the operative word; my ovaries were clearly not up to the job. After three years of failure, floods of tears, bucket-loads of envy towards pregnant people and unanswered prayers, I went to the infertility clinic at the Johannesburg General Hospital.

My envy of pregnant women was directly aimed at my dear friend Gail, from Club 7, who had married Kevin a couple of years earlier. She was one of the most beautiful women in all the world, inside and out, so gentle, kind and wise. So flaming fertile. I could hardly congratulate her when I heard she was pregnant. I threw an inner tantrum and yelled at God and the world with the question that never has an answer – why me?

This was nothing compared to the fecundity of my sister, Jenny, the fruit salad maker. Jennifer was a bony bookworm as a child and awfully annoying when I was a young, self-centred teenager. A complex character, she exploded into her teen years like a flare into midnight skies, taking everyone by surprise. She was the full Monty, having both brains and beauty. She met her first husband whilst they were still teenagers at a rehab house in Johannesburg and within a short space of time got married.

Not long after, they were involved in a horrible motorbike accident and both of them were badly injured, Jenny suffering grievous bodily trauma. They were strung up in hospital, wrapped like mummies, limbs raised and askew – it was a scene from Carry On Doctor. To continue recovery they moved to my parents' home, still strung up like marionettes. And she fell pregnant!

My bitterness knew no bounds.

Infertility is not for the squeamish. My body was invaded by alien instruments time after time, scraping, poking, pricking, scratching and prodding. I had dye injected into my uterus to check if my tubes were working, to find that only one tube was open and my ovaries didn't look too healthy anyway. Vials upon vials of blood were drawn from my pin-cushion arms and my thyroid was declared under-active.

Then, at last, morning sickness kicked in. Four years on, I was pregnant.

Morning sickness turned into all-day sickness and the only thing that could keep it at bay for a short while was Fanta Orange and cheap ham. It's a wonder James didn't come out perma-tanned.

Giving birth for the first time is, I imagine, like going into outer space on a jet-pack. You have no idea if your equipment is up to it, there is no going back after launching into the unknown and an alien is about to exit your body.

I had read all about labour and knew exactly what to do, until the time came to do it. As I was at a teaching hospital, I had a gaggle of trainee doctors surrounding the foot of the bed, peering at my nether regions as the lecturer discussed my privates most un-privately. My waters had not yet broken so one bespectacled junior, who was so young he still had bum-fluff on his face, was instructed to burst my uterus. He approached me with a contraption that looked like a rusty old wire coat hanger snitched from my granny's cupboard. He was shaking so much as he neared the point of no return that I had to reassure him. No, I did not mind being pierced up the hoo-ha with a vibrating piece of metal at all. Please, feel free.

I was aware of the transition phase and the craziness it could bring forth and was afraid I was going to swear at my husband. As it was, I only, glassy-eyed, passed him a splendid turd and he, equally glassy-eyed, reverently accepted it. They never tell you about this in the books.

After seven hours of labour James finally arrived, welcomed by a green-tinged daddy and a triumphant new mummy.

My second birth was different. Again, conceiving was difficult but nearly three years later I was expecting a baby. Or a giant pumpkin, it was hard to tell. I was so big at six months people avoided me in the streets in case I popped then and there. The baby was very happy to stay put, growing and feeding like a scene from Little Shop of Horrors ...Feed me Seymour! It was a glimpse of the future as one day he would star as the evil dentist in this very same production. Two weeks after due date when I could no longer waddle, our family doctor, Dr Shein, induced me.

Induction was great. I was able to watch the monitor attached to my monstrous belly and time my breathing according to contractions. It was all jolly hard work but only three hours long and pretty much pain-free. It helped that Richard was 10.5 pounds and practically crawled out into the world. His blue eyes looked straight through us as he cried lustily, outraged at the indignity of it all.

* * *

Family life was true to Northern Suburbs norms. Too many costs and too little money. Too many unattainable aspirations linked with consumerism and possessions. Performance equalling worth, outward wealth equalling inner riches. Perfection at any price.

Amongst all of this were the joys and ordeals of bringing up a family within a large extended family where child-rearing principles differed widely. My mother was the hub of the family. By then she had changed her name to Bobbie to indicate her own personal growth and to tell the world she was a person in her own right. She staked herself in the middle of the family playground and tethered everyone to her. She held the ties firm until someone upset or displeased her. She slackened the hold then but never ever let go of a loved one. She reigned supreme. She played a pivotal role in all the grandchildren's lives and they loved her excessively. My parents took them on seaside holidays and to game reserves, to the cinema and to restaurants. In later years my dad patted the grandkids' heads when he saw them and had little chats before turning back to his sports watching or crosswords. My mum continued to rule everyone from her lounge chair.

My husband Alan was the dark, silent type and I loved his stillness and his connection to nature. His actions spoke louder than his words and he made himself useful to others in whichever way he could. However, socially he was awkward beyond measure. He couldn't small-talk, engage in group conversations or feel relaxed at social events. He missed family get-togethers, left parties early, hated speaking on the phone and shut down emotionally when overcome by occasions.

Even so, he loved his family and we visited fairly often with his sisters and his mum. His relationship with his mother was complicated but he clearly loved her and tried his best to communicate with her. She lived with us for a short while after she sold the family home and this time was fraught with tension. Due to the difficulties linked to his Aspergers condition he did not know how to engage in a relaxed way with her or communicate his thoughts. He already controlled me and the children through his behaviour and he tried to do the same with his mum. I was too busy as a young mother, too fearful and too immature to know how to make it all work.

When she moved out of our home and into a retirement village we visited a few times before she became ill and was taken to hospital. I remember the last time I spoke to her in hospital. It was a gentle, loving time. We spoke about our plans for the future. She was going to write her children's book and I was going to illustrate it. We worked out the story line and laughed about how the illustrations should look. I kissed her on the cheek and left. It was the last time I would see her.

Alan became even more withdrawn than usual thereafter. He stopped visiting his family and stopped me from making arrangements to see them or talk to them. He refused to take me to visit his mum any more, lying about how she was, pretending he was in contact with her. I did my normal thing and obeyed his wishes. He couldn't even tell me when his mum died, just said I wasn't to go and visit her again until he made a plan to do so. Three months after she died I received a call from one of my sister's-in-law who was furious and upset that we hadn't bothered to go to the funeral. It was the first I had heard of her death.

Alan didn't express himself adequately most of the time and berated himself for not having the words. He was also dyslexic so expressing himself in writing was not an option. When we did go out with friends or family, he often sat silently for the entire evening, which annoyed and puzzled hosts no end. He was considered rude and uninterested in others present, yet when I asked him if he'd enjoyed himself his face lit up and he'd say he'd loved the evening.

His thought patterns were different to mine. Over time I got to understand how to get information out of him and how to relay information back to him in a way we both understood.

His anger at himself projected onto me and the children. We were his life and he absolutely adored us but he hated himself. He didn't want his children suffering as he did so he tried to make them perfect. He was too strict, his physical punishment was too harsh and his expectations were too high. His anger and self-hatred translated into suicidal thoughts frequently and he attempted to kill himself at least twenty times during the twenty four years we were married.

His insecurity meant he needed to be in control of us, his beloved wife and children. He affected this control by using physical force, playing mind games and by retreating within himself.

In-between all the above he was a loving and kind father, a generous lover, an amazingly supportive husband and an outdoor adventurer.

He was the kind of man who took in an abandoned baby of another race – not the done thing even in the so-called New South Africa – and gave her a family. He was also the kind of man who was unselfishly brave.

Once, we visited our friends Karin and Craig who lived in Douglasdale. It was night time and we went in our Kombi, laden with Alan's work tools. I was recovering from a break-down and this was my first night out. Pulling into their gated driveway we were held at gunpoint by four men. They forced our friends to open the gate and us to drive through. They then told us to lie on the ground, face down. The gun shook constantly as one man held it to my head and told me to give him my wedding jewellery. Alan was lying beside me and when he saw this he placed himself on top of me and said to the hijacker, 'Don't hurt her, do what you want to me, she's been sick, just don't hurt her.' He literally laid down his life for me.

We had an extraordinarily complex relationship.

Aspergers and dyslexia were not spoken about in South Africa during our time there. Alan did not have a diagnosis of either and this made his school and working life extremely challenging.

As James was growing up, I noticed many similarities in their natures and in their relationships with others. However, it was only when James was diagnosed at twenty-one with Aspergers, a form of autism, that it all made sense. Autism was to play a key role in our marriage, my total nervous break-down and in our marriage break-up.

Mission

Alan and I were members of Bryanston Baptist Church, which later became Bryanston New Covenant Church. Our lives and those of our children revolved around the church, its activities and its teachings. Our experiences there over twenty years, mine particularly, both made us and broke us. Disillusionment, hurt and bitter after-effects of too much control would follow in the latter years of membership but for many years we were loved, experiencing deep avenues of worship, laughing and crying with friends as we joined each other in serving the local and outlying communities. We saw a tiny group of people expand into a church of over a thousand and I loved being part of that growth.

Mission was a focus for the church and I felt a strong call to help or serve others. Teams went into various parts of urban and rural South Africa to preach, serve, teach, train and support those who requested it. I am forever grateful for the opportunities I had to connect with different people groups; they enriched me and I always went away convinced I had gained more from time spent with them than they had gained from me.

My friend Valerie taught me much about mission. She didn't just do mission, she lived it, she got hurt by it, she was broken by it, she survived it and left a lasting legacy. Val was a talented journalist and a single mother of a young daughter. We had been friends for years and she both terrified and amused me. She is super-intelligent, her wit is as sharp as a tiger's tooth and she can give someone a tongue-lashing that is akin to being whipped with a cat-o-nine-tails. She also has the heartiest laugh and biggest heart in the world.

She decided to move to Sekhukhune in Venda, a homeland area set up in 1962 by the South African Government in the north east of South Africa close to the Zimbabwe border. Amalgamated into South Africa in 1994, at the time Val moved there it was proclaimed as an unrecognised, independent republic. This was apartheid in all its purity and living amongst a rural Black population was an enormous risk to her own reputation and a worry for those who loved her.

With very little money she set up home and a school and went about making friends and ultimately, becoming family, with her fellow villagers. I went to visit her there and was astonished at her fortitude and her ability to get the job done with almost no resources. I stayed in the brick home of one of her friends. This home was special as it had a full bathroom fitted. Unfortunately it wasn't functional as there was no water supply but it was a thing of beauty amongst the hills of Venda.

Toilets were of the long-drop variety and to get to the little outhouse I had to wind my way through chickens scrabbling in the dirt yard. There is a simple, stark beauty to Venda and I could see myself living out my days wrapped up in a blanket like a local, sitting on a front step enjoying the open, quiet vista. Of course, in actuality the challenges involved were immense and Valerie faced them headlong.

Valerie never lost her pioneering spirit. A few years after her Venda venture she started chatting online to a bloke who lived near Seattle, America, and as they got on so well, thought it a good idea to fly out and meet him. She married him forthwith. They live in Kennewick on a farm and she drives tractors, farms cattle, raises chickens, rescues dogs and writes a blog.

She writes in one of her blogs about the cost of caring, the cost of mission and the cost of kindness. I cannot say it better than this.

When your best is not enough, April 13, 2015

Blog, American Soustannie

Himself (Valerie's husband) and I spent most of yesterday driving around 300 miles to help a scrap of a dog get home. We were just one small part of a big effort. To get Jane from Denver, Colorado to Spokane, Washington involved 14 drivers working in relay, after hours of intensive work by the coordinator who put the project together.

It feels pretty special to be part of something like that. Yes, you can argue, "Why put so much effort into one puppy when there are so many in desperate need?" And yes, maybe, differently managed, that same amount of human love, time and energy, not to mention the cost of the gas alone, could have been directed into saving a whole lot of dogs – or whales – or children.

I heard the same argument back when I ran a mission school in South Africa. I often asked people I met to make a small donation, or maybe sponsor just one child. The cost of sponsorship was equivalent to maybe one fast food meal for four, once a month. Several times wealthy people, who routinely spent more on a single dinner out than the families I served spent on a month of eating, replied, "But what's the point? There are so many kids like that – I can't change anything."

The argument is valid, but it misses the point completely. We can't change the whole world, but anyone can touch a life. As long as you stay safely outside the war zone of life, you can think in abstract terms and pray for world peace and argue on Facebook about which political party "cares" more. But, with heartfelt apologies to the Democrats and Republicans out there, no government program will magic away poverty, and nor will setting the market free enable everyone to pursue life, liberty or happiness. There is no global solution to the problem of human failure and imperfection.

If you want the world to be better, you have to make that happen yourself, one act of kindness at a time. And I honestly believe it doesn't matter whether you direct your kindness toward a kid or a puppy or [Insert Cause Here]. Any act – large or small – that adds to the sum total of happiness, peace and beauty in the world is worthwhile. One of the best things to happen to me this year was when I was having a rough day, dealing with physical pain and a whole lot of sadness, and the guy ahead of me in the Dutch Brothers drive-through paid for my coffee. He didn't save the world or change my life, but he transformed that one day for me, and while he has certainly forgotten the few dollars it cost him, I still remember how good that coffee tasted, and how it warmed my heart.

Sometimes a few dollars, or a bit of time, is all it takes. Sometimes it's more about a change of attitude. Sometimes you get to take on something big.

Sometimes it costs a whole lot more than you bargained for. I have been trying for months to write about what it was like to create a dog rescue organization, and pour everything I had into running it, and finally – just as I broke beyond repair under the strain – to hand it off to people I trusted, and then to find that my trust had been misplaced. But writing about that kept leading to what it felt like to start a school out of nothing but a gang of children, and pour everything I had into running it, and finally to break when people I trusted turned against me. I wanted to write about what it's like for your best never to be enough, about the pain of broken trust and shattered dreams, and also about the soul-scorch of burnout.

Here's the thing about burnout: you hold it at bay for as long as you can, because the need – whatever it is – is unrelenting. You feel the heat, you know you won't hold out forever, but you keep going in an effort to save what you can while you can. When you finally quit, you think that at last you're free. That's when you find out that all that's been holding you together is the purpose that has also been devouring you from the inside out. Rid yourself of the purpose, and whatever is left collapses upon itself.

So I wanted to write about that, but I couldn't figure out how to do so without sounding like I was whining or – worse – looking for a pat on the head. And while that might have been the case a year or even six months ago, whines and pats are irrelevant now that I'm through the pain.

I've just realized that what I want to write about is the fact that sometimes the cost of kindness is so high it seems to bankrupt you – but it's still worth it.

Don't get me wrong: it sucks when you take on something too big, and it eats you alive and hacks you up and leaves the remnants lying in the dirt. Burnout sucks, and being disappointed or betrayed or blamed sucks, and feeling guilty and ashamed because you know your personal flaws contributed to the crash-and-burn sucks most of all.

But it doesn't suck enough not to risk it. I believe the key to riches is to give fearlessly whenever you see a need and have the capacity to respond, no matter how little you're able to give. A small act of kindness may be to humanity like the perfectly timed flap of a butterfly's wing – and even if it isn't, it will still give wings to that one moment. And if you are blessed to have the freedom and opportunity to pour yourself out, do so with a lavish hand – because that may indeed change a small corner of the world, and it will certainly transform you.

The truth – my post-burnout truth – is that there are a whole lot of alive-minded young people out there whose kids call me granny. One of them, a girl who grew up in unimaginable poverty, is a qualified and highly paid engineer who now helps support my parents. Another is a musician, some are teachers, a few are entrepreneurs. One is a single mom who occasionally needs help with her kids' school expenses. Also, hundreds of dogs and people are happy because we brought them together, and the rescue Himself and I started is still the best in our town and doing just fine without us.

Sometimes your best just is not enough, and then failure or burnout may strike with all the devastating effect of a forest fire. But time passes, you begin to heal, and the desire to re-engage rises like sap in a young tree. And then you take a deep breath, and you do the next best thing. Maybe you can't plunge in too deep, because you've grown wary and the burns still hurt. But you can buy one child a study aid, you can help out one cash-strapped shopper at the till, you can give one puppy a ride home.

Mission in a nutshell.

Back in Johannesburg, I taught at the church pre-school which had been set up by a woman of quiet strength and vision. It was my petri-dish for a time of personal growth and development. A place too, where my teaching skills improved and my confidence soared. Teaching here enabled me to take part in many local rural and urban training times as well as my first overseas mission forays to the Far East. It was also a platform to the new chapter in our lives, The Philippines.

The pre-school decided to teach around the theme of countries and each teacher could choose a country to research and then explore with the children. I can't remember why, but I started looking at the Philippines, a nation about which I knew absolutely nothing. It fascinated me and by the end of the theme the far-away islands had crept into my mind and my imagination. I had to go and see it for myself.

The Philippines

There are over seven thousand islands making up The Philippines. Choosing to go to this country was one thing but where on earth should we go within it? Whilst on a trip to Singapore and Hong Kong, Alan and I decided to fly to Manila and check out the opportunities for me to start or support a school.

Arriving at Manila airport was a culture shock all by itself. The heat wrapped itself around me like a knitted scarf and the hubbub made me block my ears. Taxi drivers yelled for business, vendors accosted us inside and outside the airport, hotel touts waved flyers advertising rooms in our faces and hundreds of jeepneys tooted discordantly as they waited for customers.

We'd booked a missionary lodging house to stay at for four days. The heat was heavily oppressive and I lay on the bed under the ceiling fan wishing for darkness to fall and the cool of the night to come. It never came. It was too hot and too sticky and I was not happy.

The next day we met a German man staying in the mission house for a week who lived on Mindoro, the island below the main island. He and his wife ran a mission complex in Aguada, a poor neighbourhood in Puerto Galera. As it happened, he was looking for someone to help with the pre-school that they had just started to set up for local children. Within days we had visited and made a commitment to return. On such co-incidences and whims is life's journey made.

So, within a short space of time, Alan and I rented out our home and departed for Manila. James and Richard, nine and six at the time, were up for adventure and excited for the plane journey. It was the bumpiest plane ride I had ever been on. Nearly fourteen hours of airsickness ensued as we rode the thermals like a bucking bronco enroute to Hong Kong. Even the crew members were green and holding barf-bags to their faces.

We spent a few days exploring Hong Kong then flew on to Manila. After a night at a Pension we caught the coach down to Batangas, a port at the lower end of Luzon. There we took a catamaran called the Si-Kat to Puerto Galera.

We settled into a little house situated next to a brook within the mission complex called Little House on the Rock. Soon however, it was nick-named Little House in the River as rainy season welcomed us to the islands.

When it rains in the tropics, sheets of water cascade from the sky in a steady downpour for days at a time. The little brook behind our house rapidly became a swirling river and overflowed, encircling the house. Mud slides wiped traditional houses off hills and paddy fields were flooded. It was steamy and hot and wet. The local women did the shopping in the village and they still did so in the floods. So my first introduction to the simple chore of grocery shopping was in a deluge. With other ladies I walked thigh-deep through flooded paddy fields, navigated muddy forest floors and tried not to trip over fallen coconuts in the coconut groves. Finally we reached the stores which were also badly affected by the rain but as they were a little higher up they stayed relatively dry. I missed Pick 'n Pay. I even missed the car guards.

Our little house was in a settlement called Valley of Joy, a compound set up by German missionaries. This sat in Aguada, a forested area near coconut groves and a short walk away from town. Families lived in basic nipa huts, small wooden houses or one-roomed concrete-block homes. Every family kept animals, mainly chickens and pigs, whilst water buffalo grazed near the neighbouring rice paddy fields. Their food was simple; rice with vegetables, pork, chicken or fish. Dishes were made using coconut milk, bananas and mangoes. Avocadoes were used in fruit salads and sweet breakfast rolls were brought around to buy every morning.

The children were beautiful. They had huge brown eyes and glossy black hair and smiles that touched heaven. A small group of children and a teacher from the village called Nati met for lessons in the grounds of the mission station. My task was to mentor her and develop the pre-school. Coming from a community that had every bell and whistle needed for setting up a pre-school into a very poor area with no funds whatsoever is a practical and a creative challenge. Only the most basic equipment was available to buy in the village anyway so we made our own resources and used nature as our learning tool.

We got to love the Filipinos with whom we worked. They were hospitable to a fault and because of their Christian mission exposure called us 'Sister Pam and Brother Alan', although, due to their accents, I was actually 'Seeeester Pun'. When I walked to the village through their settlement the kids ran alongside me shouting and waving and calling out 'Seeeester Pun!' I felt like a jungle celebrity.

The boys went to school at Chocolate House, a small school of only six pupils, perched on top of a cliff with a view over the sea. They set off in the mornings through the forest with their cases in hand, dappled by sunlight and dwarfed by tall trees. Passing grazing water buffalo near paddy fields, they made their way into the village to catch a tricycle to school.

One day a few villagers told us that they'd seen James and Richard on a banca (outrigger boat) in one of the coves in the morning. Turned out they'd played hooky with two friends, setting out to sea in a banca and the whole village knew about it. They were thoroughly caught out.

One thing we were sad to leave behind in Johannesburg was Richard's dance studio. Lorna Rood, a dinky little ballet dancer with two small children, decided to start her dance school in Fourways Gardens, an exclusive enclosed suburb near to where we lived. Rich did his first ballet exams with her at the age of five. He absolutely loved to dance but coming to the Philippines had put a stop to that. I knew that there were starving children all over the world I could pray for but instead I sent up a cheeky prayer before we left South Africa to ask for a ballet teacher in Puerto Galera.

Sometimes I just don't expect an actual answer to my unanswerable prayers. However, once we had settled in to village life we met a tall, handsome Filipino man called Kaloy. He carried himself gracefully, his waist-long black hair shimmering down his back. He was a ballet dancer and had just finished a stint with the Ballet Philippines Company before moving back to his home, Puerto Galera, to start a studio. Rich was one of his first students. Lessons were held in a wooden house with open walls and nipa roofing, a simple studio which was a far cry from Fourways Gardens, but even more special in its simplicity.

Our friend Ingrid came to visit us from Johannesburg, bringing gifts and love from people back home. While she was there Richard fell ill with dengue fever. He became feverish, his temperature reached over forty degrees and his cheeks became bright red and puffy. His eyes turned into slits as his face swelled and he could not eat or speak. He started bleeding from his nose. It was terrifying. The local doctor said there was nothing we could do for him. He would either get well or not.

We sat on our porch, helplessly watching Richard lying on a wooden bench looking wretched. We phoned a pastor of our church in Johannesburg and asked them to pray for him. The Sunday service was just about to start over there so he told everyone about the call he'd had and the whole church, nearly nine hundred people, stood up to pray. We only learned of the corporate prayer later but as we sat on the porch, there was a dramatic change in Richard. He sat up and said he was hungry. His face had returned to normal, his temperature had dropped and his nose no longer bled. It was a visible miracle.

Dengue fever is caused by a bite from a day-time mosquito, there is no anti-viral treatment available and it can be fatal.

Medical traumas continued as Alan got a blister on the palm of his left hand after using a machete. Blisters were not good news in the tropics as they could become septic very quickly. Although Alan coated the blister with Betadine for days on end it continued to grow until it was nearly half an inch high and an inch in diameter. His fingers swelled fatly, looking like a rosy bunch of bananas. The swelling started spreading down his hand to his wrist and then towards his elbow.

Alan's wedding ring cut into his flesh, turning his ring finger purple. The pain was unbearable so we had to operate. Late one night, when the generator had long been turned off, we sat with a torch and his Swiss army knife and started sawing. We discovered that a solid gold ring takes a very long time to wear down. Four extremely painful hours later, the ring was cut from his finger.

He went to the doctor the next day who told him in no uncertain terms that he had to go hospital immediately. This was a wonderful idea except it meant we had to go up to Manila, which involved a jeepney journey, a two hour ferry ride, a four hour coach ride and then more jeepney journeys to try to find a hospital that would treat him. We ended up at the Seventh Day Adventist Hospital which wasn't fancy by any means but it still cost a bomb at foreigner's rates.

The doctors admitted him right away, diagnosing severe cellulitis. The swelling had reached beyond his elbow, nearing his shoulder. They said if he'd waited another day without treatment the cellulitis would have reached his heart and he would have died.

So he was put into a general ward, drips attached to both arms which were raised as if he was surrendering at gunpoint. It did look very comical and was very reminiscent of our days in South Africa. In most Filipino hospitals for the masses, family had to come in and help care for you, bring you food and keep you company. The ward was like a bus station, people came and went all day long and smells of home cooked food hung heavy in the humid air. As he couldn't use his hands, I had to feed Alan and help him with his ablutions. We were the only Westerners there and provided light entertainment for the sick and their families. Everyone stopped their chatter every time Alan shuffled along to the shower dressed only in his boxers, drip poles dragging and hands held high in surrender.

After a few days the infection had gone and we returned to Puerto Galera, happy that Alan had not met his Maker just yet.

Hans, on the other hand, did meet his Maker soon after we got back. Hans was a German in his mid-sixties and like millions of older Western men, had come to live in the Philippines. These men didn't come for the mangoes or the chicken adobo or the coconut palms – they came for the women. The usually had no luck in their home countries (normally one could see why just by looking at them) but they got lucky in The Philippines because Westerners were seen as a way out of poverty. They linked up with young women barely out of their teens or went for slightly older women who would become their escorts for a period of time.

Hans was adored by the prostitutes in Puerto Galera and beloved by the owners of drinking dens. He was often seen staggering up the main town street, leaning on a girl, as he moved from bar to bar. He was always cheerful even when he could hardly see out of his booze-soaked eyes. Sadly, his liver wasn't that happy and opted out of trying to sieve out all the copious amounts of alcohol running through it every day. Hans died.

His funeral was held at the large Catholic Church at the top of the main road. Hans was laid to rest at the funeral home at the bottom of the road and embalmed by the owner. The embalmer was also the butcher and the postman so he was a man of many talents. A number of people gathered at the funeral home, drinks in hand to say goodbye. This small crowd followed the coffin, held up by six men, up the road towards the church, weeping and wailing and singing drinking songs. Most of the wailers were the local prostitutes who were dressed in working gear to honour their drinking buddy and they made a colourful, eye-catching display as they swayed and sashayed up the road.

In church, the priest intoned the liturgy and sprinkled holy water on the coffin. It was probably too late for this to make a difference to Hans but I guess we all live, and die, in hope.

After the service concluded, the six men took up their pall-bearer positions and marched out the church towards the graveyard, followed by the eclectic crowd. Whooping and hollering and praising the Lord we snaked our way to the hilly cemetery. Pre-funeral drinks had caught up with everyone and it turned into a rather jolly occasion. Reaching the graves, the pall-bearers had to hop, skip and jump over tombstones to get to the appointed site. It was a tricky business, trying to manoeuvre drunkenly through the overgrown gravesite whilst trying to not upset the spirits of the underworld residents and it all started to go horribly wrong.

During one slippery leap from grave stone to grave stone, parts of Hans flew out of the coffin. A foot and a floppy hand popped out of the coffin and the mourners screamed. Children fled like mountain goats out of the cemetery and grown men shrieked. They hurriedly put Hans down and shoved his escaping limbs back into his box, beating down nails that had eased out during the procession. Burying him quickly, they dashed back to the bar to steady their nerves and to give him a rousing farewell wake.

* * *

Shopping in Puerto Galera was a social endeavour and could never be done quickly, even less so during the midday heat. Shops were small and overcrowded with goods. Store-keepers, their friends and their family members lounged around in sweltering temperatures, rising sleepily from their torpor when a customer arrived. I had to learn how to shop differently. I didn't have to buy entire packs of stuff. Here, I could ask for two painkillers, a cup of rice, half a pack of biscuits, three eggs or whatever else I needed. Eggs were difficult to keep safe on the walk home as the number you wanted were popped into little clear plastic bags for carrying.

The market was a feast of fruit, vegetables, fish, meat, rice, coconuts, sweet cakes and cassava rolls. Enormous piles of tiny salted fish lay in pyramids, flies buzzing around them lazily. When they were fried they stank most disgustingly but tasted fantastic with rice.

I had to do an emergency shop one day just outside of town. We were on top of the cliffs near an old lighthouse and my dreaded Aunty came to visit. My mother used to say that was a polite way to say you had a period. Or you could say you were visiting the Red Sea. I'll stick with my Aunty for the purposes of this story.

Having no provisions at hand to deal with Aunty's demands I went to the only shop in the fairly uninhabited area, a family-run general dealers in a private home. Most Filipinos speak at least a smattering of English but this lot did not and I spoke even less Tagalog. Trying to ask for sanitary products through the medium of mime is pretty indelicate. The shop was stuffed with so many items I could not see what I needed so sign language it had to be.

This was a topic I had never mimed before while playing Charades but I gave it a go.

With lots of understanding nods I was handed, in succession:

- a face cloth

- a toilet roll

- a box of tissues

- a hand towel

- a remedy for diarrhoea

- a roll of bandages

-and most alarmingly, a pack of cigarettes

I reverted to method acting. I had to dig deep into my thespian soul. I will not recount how I acted out my need but it was a success. With a flourish amid many nods and grins I was handed a pack of cheap sanitary towels. Changing in the shop's shower cubicle, I was amazed. The pads were huge, high and long and plasticky with wings. I had never seen wings on a pad before. I walked bow-legged to the waiting jeepney, pad rustling crisply in the cliff-top air, feeling like there was a flipping Boeing between my legs.

The other interesting thing about life in the tropics is the cockroaches.

They are a mutation of the normal little roach that I used to see when we lived in Durban. Filipino roaches are like mini dinosaurs. When the generator went off at night time there would be silence for five minutes. Then, the patter of millions of tiny feet was heard as cockroaches emerged like an army out of every crevice in the house. Going to the toilet in the middle of the night made my heart thud with fear. I switched on the torch and shone the light in a pathway to the toilet. All the cockroaches froze for a milli-second then dashed out of sight. There were always a couple still lurking around the toilet bowl so whilst in action my feet were up in the air until the awful scamper back to bed.

There was more exciting toilet action in another house in which we stayed during our second year. A family called the Duffields from our church arrived to join us on the island. We rented two simple flats with a shared verandah built right on the edge of a beautiful bay. Our flat was essentially one room with a separate shower cubicle.

The small cubicle was tiled and had a low, toilet bowl with no lid or seat and a large plastic bucket filled with water next to it. A jug was placed inside this bucket to scoop up water and splash it down the toilet to flush it. It was also used to throw water over your body instead of a using a proper shower. It was functional. At one corner of the floor was a hole the size of a saucer where water drained out. One day, I was sitting on the bowl with my knees near my ears when an exceedingly big crab started emerging from the hole, claw by claw. I was petrified of crabs and this was a monster. His eyes, twizzling on stalks, peered at me and he waved his claws at me in a very threatening manner. He did a tap dance on the tiles as he heaved his armour-clad body out of the hole. I still do not know how I did it but in an instant I found myself on the other side of the closed door with my shorts around my ankles, hyperventilating hysterically.

We were in this house when the earthquake, 7.1 on the Richter scale, occurred. At three fifteen in the morning we were woken up by a rolling, deep, thunderous sound. This was followed by an almighty shaking, like the world was ripping apart. We all shot out of the room and stood in shock, looking at the moonlit bay in front of us. Another quake hit and buildings shook, roofs fell off and people started running towards higher ground. We were all so scared we could not move. We were completely at the mercy of the elements and could only watch and wait. It was then the bay emptied out, like a plug had been pulled out at sea. We heard a loud sucking motion and watched the sea disappear, revealing the sea bed. After a short while the sea rushed in again, boiling back over the sea bed, uplifting small boats and bancas and encroaching onto our home. This happened twice more before the sea settled back into its usual rhythm.

We learned later that a substantial tsunami had formed and had headed towards our bay before veering to the right and wiping out villages fifteen miles to the east of us. For three months after the earthquake we still suffered from aftershocks and each time we heard the familiar rumble we'd dive for cover.

The 1994 Mindoro earthquake occurred at 03:15:30 PST on November 15 near Mindoro, the Philippines. It had a moment magnitude of 7.1 and a maximum Mercalli intensity of VII (Very strong). The earthquake generated a tsunami, which affected Mindoro, the Verde Island, the Baco Islands and Luzon.

Continuing with the toilet theme there are times you just have to go, regardless of the conditions. I delivered a training session to lay teachers in a slum area of Manila and was asked to speak at a local church meeting afterwards. Walking through slums is sobering. Children ran alongside us as we stepped over open sewage gutters and ducked through tiny alleys bordered by flimsy shacks. Stray dogs roamed freely, sniffing out rancid meat to eat. The humidity was intense and everyone I saw used face towels constantly to wipe sweat off their faces.

Knowing I needed a 'comfort room', the woman leading me through the slums stopped at a strange little structure. Four tall wooden posts were sunk into the ground and had black plastic sheeting strung between them to act as walls. Inside, on top of a small concrete square, stood the usual low toilet bowl and a bucket of water to use for flushing. Opening one of the flaps, she indicated I should wait a moment and I could immediately see why. The bowl edge and rim was covered in faeces. 'Never mind!' she cried, taking her flip-flop off her foot and swishing her bare foot all over the seat, wiping it clean. She then wiped her foot on the cement floor and slid it back into her flip-flop. It would be churlish to refuse a comfort stop after all her efforts so I pulled the black plastic walls closed only to realize there were great big gaps on every side. As I hovered over the bowl I was uncomfortably aware of little children peeking through the gaps, thrilled with the sight of this strange Westerner doing her stuff in their public convenience. Basic bodily functions are a great leveller.

For some of our second year we lived in a resort called Coral Cove. Alan had met the owner on the Puerto Galera pier one day. His name was Bill and he was an Englishman who had sailed the seven seas and had decided to settle in a small corner of Paradise. He let us use a flat with wood and marble finishes that overlooked a wide bay. The beauty took my breath away. Coral reefs lay close by, palm trees edged the white beach and exotic foliage bloomed vibrantly in the tropical sunshine.

The first time Bill came into our flat after we'd moved in, he wandered around looking at the photos of my family I had stuck up on a wall. Staring at one particular photo, he stopped, pointed at the man in the photo and said he knew that man. Yeah, right. I said he couldn't possibly know him as he was my dad. He insisted he knew him quite well as Jim, my dad, had been his boss! Turns out Bill had worked for my dad's company, Simon-Carves Ltd in Johannesburg about ten years beforehand. Alan had worked there at the same time and we had never met him. Given there are over seven thousand islands in The Philippines this coincidence was pretty incredible.

Bill became an instant friend. We bonded over Scrabble (which I usually won) and over evening drinks on the balcony overlooking the water. His sense of humour tickled me and his blue eyes twinkled in his sun-tanned face as he told appalling joke after appalling joke after too many beers.

His Filipina partner had two children, one of whom called Maan (Maria), lived with them at the resort. She was the same age as Richard and as cute as a button. Rich and Maan formed a friendship that lasted all his days. Bill adored this little girl, at the same time missing his older teenage daughter who lived in England and Maan knew exactly how to twist him around her little finger.

Bill snuck into my heart despite his poor Scrabble score and we have remained friends ever since. He was a real support for me when we stayed at the resort, when Alan and I divorced and during other key moments of my life. Years later I was instrumental in him getting him a job with the Brighton architects where I worked. They sent him to Libya to work, which I felt was karma for all the bad jokes he had ever told, as not too long into his contract there, Libya imploded and he and his family had to flee.

Someone else who captured our hearts was an effervescent young Australian called Zoe, who burst into the resort and blew all us all away with her infectious laughter. She stayed at the resort for a while, helping Bill with guests and odd tasks and keeping me, Alan, Richard and James in stitches the rest of the time. One favourite family activity was going into town with her to buy a small loaf of banana bread to take onto the cliffs and have a minimalistic picnic. Zoe is, quite simply, joy with skin on.

During this time the Duffields and I started a school. We walked around all the barangays (small districts or wards) advertising our school and soon gathered a small group of students. It was difficult work but very rewarding. After we left the island, the Duffields continued growing the school, called School of the Nations, and started a church. Under new management, this school today has developed into a fully-fledged College, an excellent school attracting a good number of students. When I think of the beginnings of the school and see the result today, I am filled with happiness.

Although we were not official missionaries or linked with a mission organisation, aspects of our life there had mission overtones. We had not gone to build a church. We had gone to serve a community using the skill set we had and to open up a way for others to come, should someone else wish to church-plant in the area. Amidst all the exciting experiences we enjoyed, there were some very difficult moments too and I realised that many others doing work in nations other than their own would be affected by these as well.

There was misunderstanding from friends, family and from some fellow church members at home as to the reason we went to The Philippines. Some people made it clear we were not 'good enough' to go. I guess we went because those who were 'good enough' wouldn't dream of uprooting their busy, important lives.

I missed the easy friendships I took for granted back home. Loneliness was a major problem. At times I was bitterly lonely, especially when marriage problems that already existed were exposed due to the pressures of living a different life within a different culture.

It was also hard being separated from family. When we were there, we had to communicate by hand-written letters until the first phone and fax machine arrived in Puerto Galera. Even so, we still had to go to the waterfront in town to get our letters or receive or send our faxes, for a price we found difficult to afford. Today Puerto Galera is part of cyber society. There is broadband, most people have mobile phones with all the apps that go with them and Facebooking and using other social media is a daily activity for residents. Puerto Galera even has its own Facebook page so communication is no longer an issue. The world has got so much smaller now and I imagine a lot of the difficulties we faced there, whether they were personal, relational or school related would not even be issues now.

Return to Riverlair

Returning to Johannesburg after our second year in Puerto Galera was even more difficult than arriving in The Philippines had been. Going to shopping malls or even just driving around the Northern suburbs disturbed me. There was so much wealth on display. I had lived in a village next to a very deprived settlement for most of my stay in Mindoro and the sheer ostentatious, pretentious way of life in which I now found myself living was difficult to handle. The pace of life was completely different and on starting life in Johannesburg once more, the pressure of constantly having to be somewhere important to do something important with someone important, was culture shock at its best.

The other thing that was very noticeable was that middle-class South Africans moaned. They whined about not having enough money for that new BMW, or enough credit to keep their children at private school and all sorts of other things that worry only moneyed people.

I wish I could say I remained frugal, thankful and enchanted with living on rice and dried fish but I acclimatised quite quickly and found myself moaning with the best of them within a short space of time. However, I did retain many lessons I learned from living amongst Filipinos who embraced life stoically and thanked God for every blessing that came their way.

I also realised how little I knew about my poorer neighbours, who lived in townships and faced indescribably difficult situations daily. The new South Africa had been born, Nelson Mandela was President, and the chasm separating rich and poor was laid open for all to see. A new Black middle-class emerged and White South Africans had one heck of a journey ahead of them. Culture shock would touch every citizen of my beautiful, adopted land, including me.

The boys started school at Sharonlea Primary School after returning from The Philippines. From being at a school called Chocolate House, perched on top of a hill overlooking the bay, to attending a suburban school in Randburg marked a pretty big change. The boys had their shoulder-length hair cut into short back and sides, they wore school uniforms and they wore proper shoes with knee-length socks. No more t-shirts, shorts and flip-slops for them. They had a certain amount of adapting to do. When Richard first saw the scholar patrol outside the school he said one thing he certainly did not want was to be in the Coastguards.

James struggled at school, his dyslexia impacting his ability to do his schoolwork. His difficulties in communicating successfully with teachers and peers began to create deep rivers of anxiety within him. His favourite TV programme at the time was Quantum Leap, starring Scott Bakula. Scott played a former scientist Sam Beckett, who finds himself trapped in time due to an experiment gone awry, which causes him to leap into the body of a different person each week and assume their physical identity.

James became more and more withdrawn, especially where school was concerned. One day, when I collected him after school he sat in the car and said, 'Mom, I feel like Sam. I'm there but nobody sees me'.

My heart broke for him and I moved him to a smaller school on our church property the very next term.

By 1996 we were living in a new housing development a block away from our church, called Riverlair. Homes there were semi-detached, compact units, each with a little garden surrounded by picket fencing. Living in close quarters within communities was a fairly new concept in Johannesburg back then. Due to soaring crime, safety was paramount so gated suburbs and developments had started to become the norm. It was a definite shift away from detached homes that had their own, walled grounds.

Johannesburg had a number of exclusive, guarded, enclosed communities for the wealthy. Riverlair was an example of a gated, guarded community built mainly for ordinary middle-class people. We had guards at our communal entrance and high walls topped by razor-wire surrounding it all. There was a swimming pool for occupants' use and a single carport under cover for every unit.

It took a while to get used to being on top of our neighbours and I think, in retrospect, it helped prepare me for living in England. Our unit was built near the bend of a river and our view was of tall eucalyptus trees, bush and river-side foliage. Every so often the river came into flood, rose right up until it seemed as if it would wash us away and roared mightily as it swept past us. It was thrilling to watch. Being next to the river did bring special visitors. The most frightening was a spider I saw on my lounge curtain. It was the size of a side plate and stuck out by at least two inches as it clung to the fabric. This black, hairy monster made me scream and call for Alan. Poor bloke – he was equally terrified but managed to get into a bucket and set it free next to the river. We identified it thereafter as a giant wandering crab spider which was harmless. Ah huh. My blood pressure didn't come down for weeks afterwards.

Another benefit of living by the riverside was hearing the Zionist Church groups singing on a Sunday. They'd settle themselves on the riverside in their traditional blue and white robes and fill the air with spiritual African chanting.

A celebrity occupied the unit at the bottom of our garden. Peggy-Sue Khumalo was the reigning Miss South Africa and she stayed there with her mother for the duration of her reign. Beauty queens were considered royalty in South Africa. Being the ultimate winner of the Miss South Africa pageant was an honour and a step into a very productive future and this beautiful girl lived right next door! We were made up.

James and Richard were completely in love with Peggy-Sue. Tall and willowy, she radiated beauty. She gave them little mementoes of her reign, signed personal bookmarks for them and chatted over the fence at every opportunity. She invited me to accompany her on a few special occasions where, as guest of honour, she hobnobbed with dignitaries and blew everyone away with her charm. When Heather came into our lives she played with her often, making her giggle. She gave her a nickname of Bongi, which means thanks.

Peggy-Sue has had an illustrious career since her reign, earning a MSc Degree in Economics from the University of Manchester in the UK and becoming an Executive at Investec SA Management Forum. She is married to a well-known radio personality and is still absolutely stunning.

When Peggy-Sue Khumalo moved out after her year of Queen-dom, my friend Jill moved in. Now my bestie was across the fence and life was even better! We were surrounded by nutty neighbours on all sides – living in our gated community was a bit like One Flew Over the Cuckoo's Nest Central. There is no time to go into every fruit-cake who inhabited our complex (and I include our family in that) but there are a couple that stand out.

The first Chairman of the Residents Association was May. She believed she ran a small country on a dictatorship basis. She tongue-lashed residents within an inch of their lives if they parked in the wrong parking space or added an un-approved feature to their unit. Woe betides any person who made excessive noise after ten or littered the pool area. Her voice was of an operatic pitch and cut through flesh and ear-drums like a knife. Her husband, Ralph, was a drinker by choice and suffered happily from selective deafness.

We had a Kiwi couple living in the complex next to May who were AMWAY agents. They were full of hearty cheer as they buttered you up. 'Come join our family!' they cried, 'you will be rich beyond your wildest dreams, you will holiday in exotic locations, you will even save money in the end as our outrageously expensive products are so brilliant you only need a dab at a time!' They were out to evangelize the world with all things AMWAY. Of course, Alan could not withstand their onslaught and he was unable to express that he thought it was all twaddle, so he signed up as one of their down-lines. Naturally, we failed to hook another fish for them so they stopped talking to us with immediate effect. There's always an up-side to failure.

An Englishman called Barry lived next door to us. A cheeky chap, Barry was extremely funny in a very eccentrically British way. His wife was an Afrikaans lady with big eyes like Bambi and dimples as deep as diamond mines. They complemented each other perfectly. They had two daughters and one day, the worst sorrow came and claimed their hearts. Their eldest daughter and her brand-new husband were returning from honeymoon when they were involved in a car accident and were both killed.

I only came to realize what that may have been like to deal with much later on in my life. At the time, I saw a family crumble, shell-shocked, their very beings blown apart by grief that strips the soul. Words failed me. I was useless at showing my sympathy. I could not understand the depths of sorrow they suffered and I could offer nothing but my love and prayers. Twenty years later I understood.

Heather

My niece Kathy, Jenny's daughter, was not the shy and retiring type. She was a tyrant by the age of two and by the age of thirteen, an assured drama queen. She was a passionate child and threw herself into all sorts of scrapes from which she needed rescuing.

She was particularly unhappy with life in the winter of 1996 and took an overdose of tablets to show her discontent. She landed up in a single bed ward in the Johannesburg General Hospital near the emergency rooms but she was not alone. Alongside one wall was a small baby cot on wheels. When we visited her we had a closer peek and saw a tiny bump under a blanket. Pulling the blanket away gently, we discovered a tiny sleeping baby, with skin as rich and glossy as perfectly tempered milk chocolate, black hair and long, silky eyelashes that fluttered as she dreamed.

We learned that she had been brought into this ward before having to go to the abandoned baby unit, eight floors up. Her Swazi mum, aged fourteen, had given birth and left her, safe and warm, in the care of the nurses, before leaving and never coming back. Born six weeks earlier, the baby was also six weeks premature but breathing well so she was not placed in an incubator after birth. The staff had moved her into this little room in case the mother returned.

We cheered Kathy up over the next couple of days but when visiting we couldn't stop cuddling and talking to the baby. She was so small, weighed 1.5 kilos and could fit neatly on my forearm, limbs hanging down, like a miniature sloth. One of my prayers for her was that God would find her a family so she would be loved and cared for. A word to the wise – be careful what you pray for.

When it came time for Kathy to go home we were in a quandary. My boys, my sister, my nieces and nephews, my mother and me had fallen in love with this baby and couldn't leave her lying there. She had to come with us. So we spoke to Social Welfare who organised that our home would be a place of safety for her and we were told we could fetch her in two days time.

And just like that, I had a daughter.

Alan was very supportive and we prepared ourselves as best we could for a new baby. Richard was nine and James was twelve so I had to learn baby-care all over again. My mother, Jenny, Kathy, Stephen and Marko – Jenny's boys - and my two boys all went to collect her from the hospital. Talk about a village caring for a child! We clattered into the ward where she was being kept to be met by the nursing staff, all in tears as they were going to miss her so very much.

Richard was so enamoured with the baby that he wanted to know if we could take more of them home with us. Before we got too carried away with adopting the entire baby unit we wrapped her up in a new baby shawl and took her home.

A name was the next item on the agenda. When pondering this, I had a vivid picture of wild heather growing on the moors of England, beautiful purple flowers flourishing amongst gorse bushes and brush. I felt God say to me that this baby was like heather, beautiful, strong, able to withstand harsh climates and stand against punishing winds. I sensed she was a survivor.

So I called her Heather.

Heather's adoption came through about nine months later. Going through the adoption procedure was soul-destroying. It was like having to pass a test that you knew you'd fail before you'd even started. We were grilled about personal religious beliefs, child-rearing techniques and trans-racial matters in quite an aggressive way and I started to wonder if I had any value at all as a mother.

Eventually, we were given a date and we drove to the Randburg Council buildings where an adoption judge awaited. He was lovely and gave us his blessing before giving us the adoption papers to sign. She was ours.

Like most trans-racial adoptees, Heather noticed early on that there were differences in appearances between her family and her. When she was two she liked role-playing her birth. Goodness knows where she acquired this birthing information. She instructed me to lie on my back on the sofa then clambered onto my tummy, curling herself up in a little ball. 'Push, Mommy, push!' she said and I had to pretend I was in labour and groan. Then, when she felt she was ready, she slipped off my tummy and landed in a heap between my knees. She was born!

Doris, my maid, looked after Heather when I worked. She tucked Heather onto her back, wrapping a blanket or cloth around them both as was the African custom. I was hopeless with girlie stuff and knew nothing about Black body care, so I was very grateful for Doris' help when it came to doing Heather's hair and creaming her skin with the best products.

I still need to apologise to Doris for running a mile when Heather had worms at the age of three. Used to treating my kids regularly for worms (a common occurrence in Africa) I had never really seen them in the light of day. Heather was riddled with them. Long and creamy, like cooked spaghetti, they oozed out of her little body by the hundreds. When she was sleeping a few hardy worms crawled out of her nose and slithered down her face. Richard liked pulling them out of her nose as they emerged and dropping them into a bucket. One morning, with Heather perched on top of the toilet I shot out the door telling Doris I was so sorry but I simply had to go to work. I can only imagine her thoughts towards me.

Heather was bendy from birth. She could manipulate and contort her body into all sorts of shapes at will. As a baby and toddler I frequently dislocated her arms from her shoulders just by picking her up. Toddling with sloping shoulders wasn't a good look and even the doctors were getting suspicious. I learned very quickly how to pop them back in and she was good to go.

She also had a weird thing happen with her eyes when she was about six months old. Entering her room to wake her up in the morning I called her name and reached down to pick her up. She turned over in bed and gazed at me. I yelped and jumped backwards. Her eyes had turned inside out! Her pupils had disappeared into her head and the bright red inside of her eyelids were now the outside. She looked like a baby zombie.

I rushed her to hospital, hiding her face in a blanket so nobody would faint with horror. The doctor smiled and said it was just a virus and she'd recover in a few days time. It was probably a good thing the adoption interrogation team didn't pop in for a surprise visit at that time.

Just before Heather turned one, I was asked if I wanted to join a small team going to the Far East. The trip would be three weeks long and I could decide if I wanted to take Heather with me or leave her with our family. On reflection, I chose to leave her at home with the joint support of Alan, my mother and Doris and jetted off to Singapore.

On a Wing and a Prayer

Our goal was to encourage a few South African church-planters who had made the Far East their home. We were also there to learn from them. As I had previously lived in The Philippines in a similar capacity I knew just how much meeting with familiar faces would mean. When we were living in Puerto Galera and friends or family arrived to visit, namely Ingrid, Doreen, Gill and Brendan, Alan and Meryl and my parents, we were buoyed up for weeks afterwards. In fact, one of my enduring memories of my parents' visit is that of my mother, dressed in a flowery frock, a floppy white hat with ribbons around the brim and court shoes, trip-tripping down a shallow river bed in the middle of the jungle, waving at all the little Filipino children like she was the Queen of England.

I travelled to Singapore a number of times and each time I visited, I loved it more. It's a city of order but also a city of vibrant colour. Walking through the airport is a delight as thousands of orchids grow in planters, cascade down from the ceiling and flourish in every conceivable nook and cranny of the building. Established parks show off exotic flowers and trees that thrive on the intense humidity. This damp heat sapped my body; moving from an air-conditioned room into the outdoors was like walking through a wall of heat. Air-con diving was employed – jumping into shops at regular intervals just so it was easy to breathe.

Singapore's famous Jurong Bird Park is full of parrots, macaws, hornbills, pelicans, storks and about five thousand other exotic bird species. During the bird show a parrot flew to me and sat on my arm until it was told to go back to its trainer. I felt honoured.

The citizens of Singapore are so kind, polite and helpful to tourists. There is a very modern brand-rich side to Singapore that tempts local and international shoppers but I could only afford a couple of curios and a Singaporean McDonald's Happy Meal on this trip. I was in missionary mode.

We spent a few days in moody, misty Hong Kong before flying to Beijing.

Beijing surprised me. I had not expected the city to be so modern, sleek and westernized. The old and new seemed to blend seamlessly together. We stayed in a four star hotel in the middle of contemporary Beijing where neon signs depicting well-known luxury brands dominated the view.

Like the song says, there were indeed a million bikes in Beijing, jostling for position. Some bikes had two or more passengers or carried loads that wobbled precariously as cyclists vied for position. Rush hour was every hour and the streets teemed with life.

One of my bucket-list dreams had been to see the Great Wall of China and I was enormously privileged to be able to visit this iconic site. Arriving at Badaling, the entrance just over forty miles northwest of Beijing, my heart sank to my sandals as I saw and heard the flagrant commercialism at this historic venue. Yelling vendors sold tourist memorabilia from hundreds of stalls. Touts called out loudly trying to sell tickets for tours and hundreds of confused tourists of all shapes, colours, creeds and tongue queued for access to the wall.

Once up on the wall, my perspective changed. It had so many stories to tell. It is said that as many as 400,000 workers died during the wall's construction, many of whom were buried within the wall itself. I wandered up and down the ancient pathway looking out over a deep gorge. The wall snaked over hills that rose majestically in the misty distance and I was captivated.

Soon after being captivated, I was horizontal. A sudden onset of vertigo had hit me as I surveyed the mystical, magical scene and realized just how high up I was. I had suffered a vertigo attack once before, in the Theatre in Pretoria when I was watching Cats. Seated up in the gods, the steep incline to the stage set me off and I had to leopard-crawl in my evening dress over theatre-goers' feet to reach the landing. Now, I lay on the floor of the wall and clutched the side, dizzy and disorientated and trying not to cry. I started bottom-shuffling downwards until a pair of Chinese tourists saw my meltdown and asked if they could help. Too scared to look up and out, I saw nothing more except for my own feet as they helped me walk back.

The highlight of the trip for me was visiting with a South African family in Mongolia who were there as unofficial missionaries. Getting to Ulan Bator from Beijing created huge opportunities for me to increase my prayer life.

We flew Chinese Air, a frightening flight for even the hardiest traveller. Several seats were missing in the plane, leaving only bolts on the floor. The stewardesses wore pancake make-up and moved stiffly, like robots. They served up lunch on a paper plate, a dry bread roll with a curly piece of brown-edged polony on the side. The pilot kept up a non-stop, high pitched Chinese commentary over the sound system which was most alarming. We never knew if we were going down, a wing had fallen off or if there was a bomb on board.

Somehow we made it and landed safely in another world. Mongolia was in a class of its own.

Russian influence was glaring. The Communist regime was no longer but to all intents and purposes Mongolia was struggling to break free. Bleak concrete high-rises dominated the city-scape, shops were poorly stocked and living standards were low. Our team stayed in a high-rise flat for the duration of our visit. The outlook was depressing and the hallway, typically, smelled like boiled cabbage and offal. The front doors of the buildings were heavy-duty industrial steel doors which kept the cold out and the smells in.

The people of Mongolia brought the colour and the life to a country in transition. Hospitable and open-hearted, they welcomed us warmly. They offered us the local version of tea, which they advised was best imbibed as a type of chicken broth as it was very far removed from tea as we knew it. It was good advice as our cup of tea was hot and salty with fat globules swimming on top. The food and drink didn't get any better from that point on.

Our team went with a church group to have a picnic in the countryside. Once out of the city I saw the beauty and scale of the landscape that still evoked Genghis Khan. Green hills rolled and undulated beneath an azure sky. Vast emerald plains swept across this magnificent canvas and crisp, clear water bubbled over stones in river beds.

We set up camp next to a stream and our hosts begun preparations for the meal. A giant milk urn was placed on top of a fire and some water was added. Unwrapping lumpy parcels came next. These contained a beast of uncertain origin, roughly chopped into large pieces and then thrown into the urn. Vegetables and some seasoning were added before a layer of flat rocks collected nearby were put on top of the stew. The urn lid was screwed down and the whole concoction left to boil for a few hours.

As we waited for it to cook, a wrestling competition was held in a leafy meadow. Wrestling is the national sport of Mongolia and everybody takes part in social events such as this. My fellow male team members declined a wrestling bout for fear of being maimed or rendered unconscious. The women then asked me if I would take on one of them. I agreed, knowing I was strong and fit and nearly twice their size. I was especially pleased to meet my opponent. She was a sweet little thing of nineteen, dressed in a floral frock and sporting a white floppy hat with a flower tucked into the hatband.

A circle formed around us and we began to stalk each other, like panthers. The crowd jeered and cheered as we feinted blows and elegantly sidestepped one another. I made my move.

That was the last move I made for thirty minutes. I didn't even see her coming. I recall being flipped into the air and spun like a Catherine Wheel just before I hit the ground with a dull thunk.

Mongolians 1, South Africa 0.

I recovered in time for lunch. All the Mongolian men gathered around the boiling urn in a tight circle and told our boys to join them. The lid was opened and one by one the hot rocks were removed and tossed to the men. Each man passed hot rocks to his neighbour as quickly as they could before their hands could burn. Hot-rocking had something to do with being manly, I believe.

Then it was time to ladle out the stew and devour it. I felt like a Flintstone as I gnawed a chunk of bone, bristle and meat like a caveman.

We also visited a nomadic family who lived in a traditional yurt far away on a deserted plain. They owned horses which grazed next door to the family home. The yurt was beautifully decorated inside with richly patterned carpets and hangings. It was cool and shadowed and we sat comfortably on stuffed, covered benches. We were then offered refreshments. A bowl filled with a white viscous liquid was presented and passed from person to person around the room. The liquid was homemade fermented mare's milk and it tastes just like it sounds. It was hard to look appreciative whilst simultaneously pursing my lips like a closed up anemone and fighting the gagging urge to forcefully return the mare's milk to said mare.

It was then time to go to Taiwan. I met extraordinary people, Westerners and Taiwanese, who inspired me with their work ethic and their spirituality. I had the opportunity to hold a team-building art workshop with church members based on a story of a scarecrow. After hearing the story of the lonely scarecrow teams built giant scarecrows from junk materials, tape and string. They were marvellous to behold and we spent time afterwards talking about the dynamics of each team and the part each individual played in the group. We also took time to explore the exceptionally noisy, industrious city.

After spending time with old friends who had relocated in order to start another church, my team went back to South Africa and I popped over to Manila for a brief visit with the Duffields, who were still living in Puerto Galera.

It was strange going back. It was lovely seeing some of my old friends in town and seeing how this little town had grown since I last saw it. The Duffields had moved to a house in Sabang, an area known for its prolific amount of bars and seedy clubs. Many Westerners lived there with Filipino wives or girlfriends whilst tourists sometimes seemed to outnumber the local populace.

The school we had started together was a hub of activity. Shane and Sandra taught children, ran the school and led a small church on site. I hoped my visit was an encouragement to the family but for me, this was a defining moment. I had played my part in this corner of the world and I knew I would not be back.

Break Down

I missed Heather's first steps while I was away. Seeing her and the boys again was wonderful but something was very wrong with me. I had been shaky and weepy at odd times during my trip and these feelings increased when I was home. I continued to shoulder too many responsibilities at home and at church and my relationship with my husband was toxic.

I was standing in the foyer of New Covenant Church when I finally broke apart. Standing with a group of friends, I was aware that I was disconnected and struggling to follow the conversation. Taking a step backwards, I saw and heard what seemed to be a corrugated iron garage door close down in front of me. I was shut in.

In that moment, I lost my mind, my strength, my soul, my hope and my future. I lost me.

Friends took me to a private home where I lay on the sofa, crying from the depths of my being, seeing nothing but blackness surrounding me. Unable to walk, they carried me to a car and took me to the emergency department at the local hospital. I was placed in the care of a psychiatrist, Dr Patrick McGraw, who admitted me to the psychiatric ward immediately.

Days of darkness followed, punctuated by drugs and sleeping pills. I could not stand to see my husband so he was banned from visiting. My mother and father took over the reins of parenting with the help of my housekeeper, Doris and I lost myself in a drug-induced stupor.

After two weeks I was released into the care of Club 7 friends Kevin and Gail, who lived in Ficksburg, a small town about four hours drive away. Bundled into the back of a Kombi, I slept fitfully as a friend drove me down to their home. Gail, a qualified and experienced nurse, looked after me in the week that followed, making sure my medication was taken and making me walk short distances to build up my strength.

This brick and mortar home became my lucky bean tree crypt. I pulled my bedroom curtains closed, letting the Free State sun shine through the fabric, encasing me in warm, golden light. I was safe.

After a week of recuperation in Ficksburg I moved into an integrated guest suite in a church member's home back in Johannesburg. I could see my children and my parents for brief visitations which caused a flicker of light in the darkness.

One day I found myself on the toilet in the bathroom, blood streaks covering the walls and seat and floor. I had no idea how it got there.

On another day I curled up in an armchair in my room and phoned the pharmacy. I needed to know how many sleeping pills I ought to take to ensure an eternal outcome. I never did get an answer as the call was cut short but I held the telephone listening to silence for a very long time.

Alan came to visit once. The one who had broken me, the one I hated, was the one I loved and the one I needed. We slept together, in my chamber of horrors, holding on to each other with fierce desperation.

Life is interesting when viewed through broken lenses. Re-entering social situations filled me with deep-seated panic. I began looking through other people's eyes again, to get some measure of control and to help me cope. When I saw myself from that perspective I was a hollow shell. It was like my heart and soul and been blown clean out of me; my frame was being held together by knot-weed and my emptiness was on show for all to see.

Breaking apart is like living death. I found my space in this world got filled up by others, those who were still whole and able to give. It didn't take long – a few months and my job and my ministries were seamlessly claimed by these intact others. I felt as if I had been wiped out of history. I was a ghost of a former time.

Discovering who I now was took an enormous amount of emotional energy and is still an on-going process more than twenty years on. My first breakthrough came after nearly a year when I realised with sudden clarity that my value was in me, simply me, and not in what I could do or accomplish. For years I had performed to please others, striving for excellence in every area. Failure meant I was not worth much. I had to do more, work harder, be nicer, become more intelligent and above all, never say no.

Once I realised that I was of inherent worth, I started saying no and healing began.

At the same time I lost my mind, my friend Jill lost her husband.

Jill

I met Jill in the late 80s and disliked her on sight. She tottered up my driveway in her clickety-clacketty high heels to fetch me for a church meeting, blonde hair bouffant and girly and hands waving around like a windmill. She had so much energy it was like being driven to church by a Duracell bunny.

However, opposites attract and we formed a quirky, close relationship marked by a shared sense of the absurd. She also introduced me to Pimms, an act of love for which I will be forever grateful.

Jill and her husband Greg had a jet-ski which they used at the Vaal Dam. On one occasion I went with them to have a go. I quickly discovered that mounting a bobbing jet-ski is even more difficult than mounting a camel. Jill took the front position at the controls. She leapt aboard lightly and called me to hop on behind her. Now there was a difference of about 30 kilos in weight between the two of us and I was totally inexperienced. This should have been thought through a bit better. Approaching the rear end of the jet-ski which was rising and falling with the ebb and flow of the water was panic-inducing. I threw myself bodily at the jet-ski, landing tummy first on the saddle with my limbs hugging this water beast with every ounce of strength I had. My substantial bottom, displayed for all to see, acted as an anchor and within seconds, my end of the jet-ski disappeared under a froth of water, the front end reared up and I slid off inelegantly into the deep.

It was not a pretty sight from the banks of the Vaal.

I had my first migraine at Jill's house. It was the start of ten years of weekly unbearable migraine attacks for me. I was sitting in her lounge breastfeeding Richard as James played with Glenn-John outdoors. Jill was making tea whilst we chatted – a process that always took forever as she could not do two things at once. There were times I'd go for tea and end up making it myself as Jill shot around the kitchen like a pinball wizard doing everything at once and achieving nothing. Suddenly, I felt a lightning bolt of pain strike the left side of my head. Immediately the left side of my body went completely numb and I could no longer hold onto Richard, who detached his mouth with a pop and slid down my lap onto the carpet.

As well as becoming numb I lost the power of speech. It was as if I was having a stroke. It took a long while for Jill to stop herself pinging around the kitchen to notice me slumped on the chair. She then took me to her bedroom, laid me down and shut the door, saying she'd look after Richard. That was a wonderful, thoughtful idea, except I thought I was dying and I could not communicate that with her. I tried shouting at her with my eyes but she just tut-tutted and closed the door. By the time she decide to check on me I was reciting the Lord's Prayer in my head, convinced I'd had a stroke and was on the way to eternity. When she finally noticed my deadpan expression and drool spilling out of my slackened mouth onto her pillows, she called the doctor in double-quick time.

My doctor, Dr Shein, was another human angel. He knew my family and me inside out, brave soul, and he knew a migraine when he saw it. He injected me with his migraine cocktail, pethidine, maxolon and voltaren. Pethidine hit me within a minute and it was like embracing a lover. I could feel it entering my body and travel swiftly up to my pain receptors. The release from my migraine pain was indescribable. I slept for hours and woke up smiling. Over the next ten years I had so many migraine cocktails my behind was as punctured as a pincushion. I inevitably developed a passion for pethidine. I was brazen in my love for this drug but sadly it stopped being quite so easy to access after that time and I had to try other medications which were never as effective.

Jill and I loved amateur dramatics. We had no shame. On one memorable occasion I did the chicken dance dressed as a giant chicken on the church stage for about eight hundred people. I don't remember what faith had to do with being a chicken but I was clucking marvellous. Jill did skits using her brilliantly executed broad South African accent to depict various characters that didn't have a brain. Our best joint skit was an act done for a friend's stork party (baby shower). We called it the Dance of the Pregnant Fairies and we choreographed a little ballet to Swan Lake music. Jill was actually pregnant at the time and her baby-bump rose majestically above the frill of the tutu. I just looked pregnant and my tummy swelled beautifully over my tutu as well. Margot Fonteyn was one of my heroes when I was growing up and I felt very close to her that day.

Jill and I loved getting away from it all. We'd pile our boys, Glenn-John, Bradley, James and Richard into a car, which was usually on its last legs, and thunder off into the distant countryside. Going to the Eastern Transvaal was one such adventure.

About one hundred kilometres outside of Johannesburg the car started behaving strangely. It was travelling steadily on flat roads but when it glimpsed a hill or even just an extended slope, it would sigh, as if the effort was all too much and stutter to a stop. We learned to let it have a little rest before firing it up again to brave the road ahead. As we approached another hill the same thing would happen, over and over again. At this rate it would take us three days to reach our destination.

The kids were getting boisterous in the back and waving a wooden spoon at them didn't have much result. The disciplinary tactic employed in those days for errant children was a whack with a wooden spoon, preferably on the posterior but in cases like this, any spot would do. So we turned into the nearest town and pulled into a mechanic's garage. The mechanic was busy but faced with a screaming carload of kids and two frazzled women, he decided to fix it then and there. He fiddled around under the bonnet for some time, exchanged some parts, sorted the problem and told us how much it had cost to fix. However, we needed to test it out on the nearest hill, before coming back and paying him.

We piled back in the car and literally headed for the hills. To our surprise, the road ran flat for another hundred kilometres. There were no hills until we reached Waterval Boven, at which point the mechanic's work was tested and the car soared beautifully up every incline. It was much too far to return to the mechanic and we still owe him his hard-earned money to this day.

We stopped at Waterval Boven (Waterfall Above), a gorge that plunged down towards Waterval Onder (Waterfall Below) and then decided to go for a walk along the ridge which was covered in bush, trees, veld flowers and grasses. The kids went one way and we went another. Our path started petering out, causing us to crab-walk at an angle so as not to slide down into oblivion. I'm not very good at crab-walking and I did indeed do the slide of terror, hurtling like a bowling ball down the cliff toward the river bed far, far below.

I was saved by a small tree hugging the cliff face. Crashing into the tree trunk I came to a sudden halt, totally disoriented and badly winded. My ankle also hurt. I contemplated getting up and climbing back up the gorge. Nope. I was too sore to move. Jill came down to where I was and helped me get up and climb back up the steep face. This was not an easy task for her as she is thin as a whippet and I am a chunky monkey, but little by little we climbed to the top.

Unfortunately at the top was a wall at least four meters high, above which was the road. There was no way I could clamber up that and Jill was exhausted after heaving me uphill so she did what comes naturally at times of crisis. She prayed. As she finished her SOS prayer, a man in a safari suit peered over the top and asked if he could help us. I had never met an angel in a safari suit but it's fair to say they do exist. He hauled me up with the help of a rope aided by Jill, who pushed me up the wall like Superwoman. We were saved!

Talking about being saved, Jill and I came to the rescue when my sister Jenny was about to give birth to Steven. Her daughter Kathy was four and they were staying at my parents' home in preparation for the new arrival. My folks were out when I got a call from Jenny saying she thought she may have started contractions and what should she do? I asked how far apart the contractions were and she said nonchalantly about a minute, maybe a minute and a half. I did not have a car to use so phoned Jill who had her two small children and her dog in the car. She drove like the famous bat out of hell and picked up me, little James and one month old Richard before flying down the highway to fetch Jenny. It was fortuitous Jill drove a station wagon. We skidded to a halt at the gates of my parents' home where Jenny was waiting with Kathy. We made a bed out of dog blankets in the back of the wagon and put Jenny on top. We then wedged the four kids and dog in the back seat and me and Richard in the passenger seat and screamed off to the hospital.

The car sounded like an asylum. Four children shrieked and fought and giggled, the baby burped, the dog barked incessantly and Jenny squawked loudly with birth pain. Even the car was backfiring.

Just in time we screeched to a halt in front of the emergency doors and helped Jenny out of the back of the wagon and onto a wheelchair. Steven was born very soon thereafter in somewhat dramatic fashion. Jenny nearly died after giving birth and gave us all a huge scare.

A few years after that, Jill's world collapsed. Her husband Greg often flew small planes to Botswana for private tourists and he set off as usual from Lanseria airport one fateful day. Sometime later, Jill got a call informing her that the plane had gone down and all aboard had been killed.

Life can change profoundly from one moment to the next. Seeing a beloved friend endure such hardship was extremely difficult. Words were inadequate so hugs and prayers and practical help had to do. She was brave and resourceful even when she was broken and slowly we learned how to live life again, she without her husband and me without my mind. It was a long journey marked by giggling hysteria and tears and in the end we both survived.

Jill was a successful agent and she introduced me to the world of property. I quit teaching and started working at Pam Golding Properties, a premier property business in South Africa. Jill and I both worked within the rentals department, dealing with exclusive properties in the Northern suburbs of Johannesburg.

Trying to be a smart businesswoman was just about beyond my remit but I did my best. Just seeing the huge amount of money changing hands was educational. Sales commissions were extremely high at 7% and the workplace was a cut-throat hive of competition. I had a lot to learn.

One interesting rental I processed was for a large, slightly ropey house in Bryanston. The lessee's name was Nimbus, which actually means a 'luminous cloud or a halo surrounding a supernatural being or a saint.' Nothing could have been further from the truth. Besides having a huge head with curly grey hair sprouting wildly in the wind (no halo could ever have fitted onto that) Nimbus had to have someone else sign his lease because all his references were dodgy.

Going to check up on the property two weeks later, I was let in by a young Thai lady who told me Nimbus was out but I could come in. My eyes surveyed the open-plan lounges, taking in exotic nymphettes of Eastern origin lazing on sofas or doing their nails in the bar area. Touring the premises revealed several rooms with massage tables, towels and lotions. There was one room that was securely locked and I was not allowed to enter. I was quite relieved as I was sure that was the S&M room, judging by a small whip resting against the door. There was an all-pervading odour of body sweat and cheap perfume in the house and I made it back to the front door just before I began to gag.

Nimbus came out on top in the end as the lessor was very happy to have a brothel in his house as long as the exorbitant rent was paid on time every month.

I got a call to view a property newly available for rent and went off to meet the owner, Jennifer. Jennifer owned a number of properties and lived on a smallholding in an exclusive outlying suburb. Now if Jennifer was named after a storm she would be a twister. She gathered energy and focus and drive within her, locked onto her goal and bore down with terrifying force to get what she wanted. She was utterly beautiful, gorgeous long hair gathered into a messy bun, her goddess figure clothed in expensive finery. I parked my car, a banged-up Nissan, next to her gleaming BMW and greeted her, feeling like a Hill-Billy.

Apparently I did my job fairly well and she was so impressed she asked if she could join me in the rental division and be my partner. Caught up in her twister trail I could not refuse.

Our partnership was marked by drama and laughter. It was also marked by a bucket-load of flirting by most of the male lessors we met. I felt as if I was Jennifer's mum and chastity belt rolled into one. Our double act helped get us deals though and sometimes we won Agent of the Month in the regular company competitions.

During one viewing, about a year after we got together, we stood outside next to a prospective tenant's car, talking about the lease. Out of the blue I felt a bit faint then felt nothing at all as I collapsed and hit the tarmac, landing with my head under the exhaust pipe.

The same thing happened a few times at work and at home and after one particularly bad incident I was taken to hospital and diagnosed with epilepsy.

Busy with a correspondence BA Communication degree, I had to give up studying just before my third-year exams. My property rental career steadily nosedived thereafter too as I couldn't drive. For months I fitted in all sorts of public places. Every shopping mall in our neighbourhood sent me into a spin, any flashing lights made my legs give way and I couldn't go anywhere without someone with me. My medication settled the fits down eventually and I knew it was time to look for work and living options elsewhere. We needed a new start. At the same time, my mother needed a new heart.

Affairs of the Heart

My mother lived with heart trouble for many years and slowly but surely it started to get the better of her. She carried her nitroglycerine tablets at all times, which she put under her tongue when having an attack. Even walking very short distances tired her and going shopping became an extremely lengthy chore. There were times we took over twenty minutes to walk down to her retirement unit from the car park, one hundred metres away. There was only one course of action to take and that was a triple bypass operation.

My mother was convinced she was going to die so she told us all in detail what she wanted to happen upon her demise. Tearfully, she made her peace with God and man and was pushed down the corridor to the operating theatre with her arms already folded across her chest as if in rigor mortis. It turned out that God was not quite ready for her so she returned to the ward after the operation hooked up to all sorts of wires and tubes and pumps that kept her breathing and away from St Peter's gate.

Once she was allowed home, I stayed with her for a few days to help her recuperate. I am not a natural nurse. I lack empathy. I am not a there-there kind of person either. The poor woman had to endure my ministrations as my father had even less nursing ability. The worst part was changing her compression stockings. These were very tight-fitting and she had to wear them after her surgery to stop blood clots developing in her legs. My mother was flat on her back in bed for a week and these blessed things had to be changed every day.

Now, my mother had two responses to everything. Laughing or crying. Often she would do them both together which was pretty confusing. Or she would laugh when in pain and cry when she was happy. She was an emotional mystery. When I changed her stockings it was painful, so she got the giggles every time I started the procedure. To do this, I had to kneel on the bed astride my mother's knees so I could grip the stocking edge. As I loomed over her, her very generous belly started shaking with suppressed laughter and tears spurted from her eyes like little fountains. I frequently lost my balance in the middle of this task and came perilously close to falling on top of my mother, which made her laugh and cry until her face turned red and her bladder burst. At the very least, the whole exercise left me sweating from every pore. It made her very happy or very sad, it was hard to tell.

Shortly after my mother returned from hospital my father thought it would be a good idea to get his ticker checked out, just in case. As luck would have it, he was found to be in urgent need of a bypass operation as well. So off he popped to hospital for the same procedure. They both compared scars and the side effects of medication. I thanked the good Lord that my father could put his own compression stockings on, no help needed.

Brighton

Both Alan and I had British heritage so we applied to move to the United Kingdom. By this time, Alan had been held up at gunpoint ten times as he was driving for work around Johannesburg. We had been hijacked in our friend's driveway and had our vehicle stolen. I was in an armed bank robbery in the Mall and our whole family had been held at gunpoint in a store. The last event was the proverbial straw on the camel's back.

We skipped church on a Sunday to spend some time as a family, window shopping at local shops and having a bite to eat at a restaurant. We went into a large computer and gadget store and moseyed around the shop. Alan held Heather whilst James was nearby looking at videos. Richard was on the other side of the store. Suddenly I saw a staff member kneel down and put his finger to his lips. He gestured for us to lie down and I looked around in puzzlement, only to see other people sinking to the floor quietly.

Then we saw the gunmen, a group of robbers armed with rifle and pistols, spreading out across the shop floor. Lying down next to a display unit, I put my mobile phone underneath so it wouldn't be taken. I was so scared that my mother would phone to have a chat – she usually picked her moments. James was pushed forwards towards us at the point of a gun but Richard was nowhere to be seen. Another robber had taken him at gunpoint to another group of shoppers far away from us. The robbers had a bit of a disagreement – should they rob the store and us? Or just take the till pickings and get out? They locked us in whilst they debated. Being held hostage is petrifying. Life was cheap in South Africa, people were killed daily and the threat of being shot was tangible. All I could think of was my children, especially Richard as I could not see him at all.

It was that this point I actually saw the light. The tunnel light. The one you see when you are going to die. I could see a warm glow beckoning me at the end of a dark tunnel and I moved towards it in my mind's eye. I knew I was going to enter another dimension and I was not afraid. I felt wholly and utterly at peace. Just then the robbers decided to rob the store, leave us alone and get out, yelling that they would shoot if anyone tried to move until they had gone. We lay frozen and unmoving until we heard the getaway Kombi race away then we rose, running to find Richard across the room.

The hijacking and all the other experiences related to our own personal safety led to severe stress and anxiety. Fear made me unable to get out of a car at night without shaking or even walk to church, one block away from our home. The only day I braved that walk ended up with me slipping on the overflow of a sewage pipe that had leaked just outside the church entrance. I felt my feet shoot out beneath me and I sailed through the air, landing face down in the slimy excrement. I lay there for a moment, stunned by the fall and the indescribably horrible smell. Gathering myself up, I sloshed out of the pool of sewage and made my way into church as it was closer than going home. I don't think 'coming to Jesus just as you are' took such whiffy circumstances into account and I was given a very wide berth until I'd cleaned up sufficiently for me to go home and have a bath.

It was definitely time to go to England.

James and I flew across a week before he turned eighteen, which was the cut-off age for a child on my Ancestral visa. We stayed with family in Middlesbrough who helped us wrap our heads around this very different culture in which we found ourselves. On the night of his birthday I took James to a Pizza Hut and we celebrated his coming of age.

Leaving James to stay in Middlesbrough, I travelled to a few different parts of England to visit friends and decide where we should settle when we finally moved. My last stop meant meeting up with Caroline, an English friend we had met in Johannesburg a few years earlier. She had quickly become part of our little family for a year. She now lived in Brighton with her husband Dean and their children. So in February, 2002, I was introduced to the cosmopolitan city of Brighton & Hove.

It was freezing. Caroline took me onto the world famous Brighton pier during the coldest month of the year. My face turned to marble and my joints seized. I couldn't feel my extremities and I wondered who on earth would choose to be outdoors in this weather. We went to Asda next to do some food shopping and the trip from the car to the entrance was excruciatingly cold. I was way out of my comfort zone. However, I fell in love with this city and decided this would be our home town.

After my recce trip I flew back to South Africa to start final preparations and say our goodbyes. The great trek had officially begun.

Alan arrived in the UK a few months before me, James joining him in Brighton. By the time Richard, Heather and I arrived in August 2002, he had let an ex-council semi-detached house for us in the suburb of Hangleton, Hove. Reunited, we moved in and started our new season of life.

Caroline and Dean led a small church in Hove and thanks to them and other members of the church, we were kitted out with the basics for living. Leaving South Africa had been financially draining as the exchange rate was R18 to £1, one of the highest ever seen. After selling our two properties in Johannesburg and paying all our costs we were left with enough money for a deposit on our rented house, three month's rent and living expenses for the next few months.

The summer holidays were nearly finished and we had a week to find schools for Richard and Heather. Richard had attended the National School of the Arts in Johannesburg when we left South Africa. He was a gifted performer but there was no way we could afford for him to go to a private arts school here. Fortunately, we discovered that our house was a few blocks away from Blatchington Mill School, a government school that specialised in Performing Arts. We contacted the school admissions team who said there was only one place left for the start of the new academic year and they allocated it to Richard.

Getting to grips with life in England was not as easy as I thought it might be. Having spent pockets of time over here over the years I imagined the transition would be simple. Also, people spoke English. How hard could this be? Extremely hard, as it turned out.

Finding a job was a major challenge. English employers were not as impressed with my CV as I was. I didn't understand English systems including health services, banking, education and transport. I was still in trauma over the security issues we'd had back in South Africa so could not cope with night falling by 4:30pm in the winter. Walking in the late afternoon terrified me. Hearing footsteps behind me would cause me to freeze and wait for the person behind to pass me, praying I would not be hit over the head or be held up at gunpoint.

I managed to get a job at a call centre in town. If hell was on earth it would look like a call centre. A huge room was divided into tiny soulless cubicles, each cubby hole having a computer screen and a telephone. A line manager barked insults and on rare occasions, congratulations, constantly over a megaphone. Failures and successes were written on a white-board for all to see. Nobody I called seemed to understand my accent so I enunciated extra clearly just to be understood. Two things happened that put paid to this job.

The first was that I had two major seizures in my cubicle within the two weeks I worked there. The emergency ambulance crew saw to me both times whilst I frothed under cubicle shelving, my legs jerking and my eyes rolling back into my skull. It was more exciting than phoning cross people to tell them they could get cheaper electricity if they just swopped providers.

The second thing that happened was that I fell down the stairs at my home. I completely misjudged the top step and slipped, bumping myself on every step with every part of my body as I careened towards the ground floor landing. Face down on the multicoloured swirly carpet, I wondered why on earth this place I now called home was called Great Britain.

Overnight my feet turned blue and my left foot's big toe flopped around like a seal trying to find its way to the ocean. A trip to A & E ended up with being admitted for an operation. My tendon had snapped and I was told if it wasn't fixed I would have back problems and it would cost the NHS much more to fix later on. So I bypassed all the waiting hip and knee replacement patients to have my tendon reattached immediately.

Drifting off in a fugue of ether, I embraced sleep and woke up a while later, with tendon successfully rejoined. What I did not expect was the level of pain emanating from my toe. It was savage and remorseless. Morphine became my best friend. I loved morphine so much I wanted it to be my forever friend but sadly, our relationship had to end when I left hospital.

I had a neon pink plaster cast from my toes to my knee and hobbled around using government-issue crutches for six weeks. It was winter, nearly Christmas, rainy, bitterly cold and pitch dark after four thirty. Catching buses and going shopping on crutches was an immense, agonising effort. Life was dismal.

Our first Christmas was not full of cheer. Money was tight and tensions were running high. Feelings of utter despair overtook me as the pressures of a difficult marriage mounted day by day. I could feel the garage door begin to descend once more as I started to unravel.

Just before Christmas we received the nine boxes of goods we had shipped over from South Africa when we left. I was so excited I started ripping open the boxes when they arrived. There were my own pots and pans, my books, photo albums and special little objects that reminded me of home and family. Their only value was sentimental and I spent the afternoon on the hallway floor surrounded by tat and soaking in memories. Alan came home from work and flew into a rage because I hadn't opened the boxes properly. Apparently I should have cut through the tape and opened them neatly.

And that is the moment when my marriage of twenty four years ended.

It came down to a choice – my health or my marriage, and I chose my health. I loved Alan but I couldn't live with him any longer.

My parents came over for New Year to stay for a couple of months, which helped me through the separation.

Our divorce was granted nine months later, a quick process due to my emotional distress caused by my spouse's 'unreasonable behaviour'. Some years later I read an article entitled 'Living with Autism' which said that studies showed living with a spouse who was on the spectrum was one of the most difficult partnerships of all to negotiate.

Children

Of all my children, James was the most complex. He struggled with communication and shared many characteristics of his father's coping skills. When James turned twenty-one, two years after the divorce, he was diagnosed with Aspergers and suddenly, it all made sense. It was like a searchlight had switched on and we could see. We could travel this journey together, him and I, and God willing, it would not be as painful as the one his dad had travelled all his life.

By now Richard was flourishing at school and immersing himself into drama and dance. He had a very wide circle of friends and often held house parties. To save himself from feeling mortified at his home and family for these events, he cleaned the house from top to bottom beforehand, hiding away all mess and ornaments of questionable taste. He then banished me, James and Heather to my bedroom upstairs, like we were lepers. To be fair, he did put a telly and snacks in there with us but we were very much persona non-grata. We had the joy of listening to girls giggling in the landing and kids vomiting up cheap wine and cider in the bathroom, which made up for feelings of isolation.

Rich had a girlfriend for a short while, a very pretty, sweet girl who clearly adored him. I told him in no uncertain terms that she was not to sleep in his room at night when she stayed over. I had standards. Girls could not stay in his bedroom, end of. My standards rapidly became very flexible a short time later.

Richard started behaving a bit oddly when he was seventeen. He'd say he was spending the night at a friend's house but this would be untrue. He spent hours at the gym in pursuit of the body beautiful. He asked if he could stop going to church with me every Sunday. He was troubled, secretive and melancholy, completely opposite to his usual character. I did the Mother Snoop and hit the payload. His email was left open on the computer in the hallway and I saw an email from a thirty year old man he knew from the gym. It was clear they were in a relationship.

My heart did cartwheels as I started realising what this meant, for him and for me.

I sat him down in his bedroom that same day and asked him to tell me what was happening in his life as he seemed troubled. He burst into tears and sobbed in my arms, unable to speak. I asked him if he was gay and he nodded. He started apologising for the hurt it would cause me and for failing God and for not being the person we thought he was. I held him close, telling him he was still my son, my beautiful son and nothing would make me love him any less.

After the tears had subsided he told me about the man from the gym. I had a bit of trouble with the age gap in all truth – even if they were straight surely this was cradle snatching? Thankfully, this man was very nice and normal and as Richard acted far older than he was, it seemed to be a good first relationship for him.

Rich's next relationship was with a boy called Brett, an Australian on a working holiday to Britain. Now the bedroom rules changed. Girls were allowed to stay in his bedroom but boys were banned. Naturally this didn't work and Brett became my third son for a while. The responsibility of being a mother of a gay child had its challenges. It was even more challenging because I was a Christian, a church-goer and a much protected South African.

Homosexuality had been preached against in every church I had attended. Our minds were made up for us, no open discussion was encouraged and we very seldom met gay people. This wasn't difficult as most gay people didn't want to come to church anyway for obvious reasons.

Now I was the mother of a gay boy. What to do? There was one non-negotiable – I would always love and support him. I then had to park my prejudice, listen, and learn to understand. There is a mourning process most parents work through when they learn their child is gay. My hopes and dreams for him in terms of finding a wife and having children had to change direction. I processed the fact that I may never have grandchildren. Rich might be lonely when he was old. He might get AIDS and die. He would be subject to other people's judgement and get hurt, emotionally and physically.

I had to rethink my belief system and be willing to walk this new road with my son. Little did I know that this journey would be a gift beyond measure.

Heather started school at West Blatchington Infant School when we arrived in the UK. She was six and as children start school in South Africa when they are seven, she was already behind in her learning. Her peers had started school when they were four so it was a long haul for her to catch up.

It was during her first few years at school that she showed an amazing knack for losing everything. Her lunch box, her jumper, her sports bag, her books all went AWOL on a regular basis. Keeping time was another difficulty. She played with her friends at the green next to our house and never remembered to come home. Teachers complained about her inability to sit still in class but she was applauded as one of the top sporting pupils in school.

She was fearless. She went for bike rides with older kids to the other side of the suburb. She jumped off piers and sea walls into crashing surf. She always somersaulted the highest out of anyone on trampolines. She never stopped moving. It was like living with a whirlwind.

Legal Aliens

My first teaching job in Brighton was at Circus Pre-school, a community pre-school aligned with a church in central Brighton. I had years of experience of working with young children under my belt and knew I would be able to just slide into teaching work here with ease. I put the calamitous call-centre working history aside, said goodbye to my neon pink cast and started my new job with a spring in my still wonky step.

Starting to teach at the pre-school was a major cultural shock for me. This was an inner city pre-school, with two rooms, a single toilet and a tiny area of decking that served as an outdoor play area. Most of the schools at which I'd taught had jungle gyms that were bigger than this. If the weather was bad we could use the hall down the corridor, which meant setting up our equipment beforehand and putting it back after use. Part of the job required us to clean the pre-school at the end of every day. Clean the pre-school? In South Africa we had staff who not only cleaned, they mixed paint, made snacks and packed away resources so that teachers could do what they knew best – teach. It is safe to say I had to climb down a peg or two in my mental approach.

I had to learn new jargon and new practices. I was now an early years practitioner at an early years setting, not a pre-school teacher at a pre-school. As such, I had to scaffold learning for the wee tykes through play. I had only heard the term scaffolding before when my house was being built. Learning through play had only been hinted at in South Africa. Most of the child's learning was due to brilliant teachers, such as me, who led learning through excellent teaching techniques before and after playtime breaks. During these play breaks teachers sat and sipped tea and chatted about their weekends.

To help me come up to speed with these new practices I had to attend Early Years courses run by the Local Education Authority. These courses were quite daunting as I wasn't au-fait with English educational jargon and I didn't know any of the other educators who were there. However, it was during one of these courses that I met up with my old Bulawayo nemesis, Morna.

As was fairly usual in those days, I had an epileptic fit at the course during the first part of the morning. I recovered to attend the afternoon session at which time a lovely, fair-haired woman came up to me and asked if my name was Pam Black. I had not been called by my maiden name for over two decades and wondered if my fit had transported me to another dimension. Morna introduced herself to me and said she'd recognized me by my profile. I am not sure whether it was the ski-slope nose or the overbite that ticked the memory box for her. She kindly refrained from mentioning my foaming mouth and jerky limbs. When she said her name I recognized her immediately and it was like coming home. We discovered we lived about ten minutes drive from each other in Hove and we instantly resumed our friendship that had started on another continent all those years ago. To my chagrin, she is still cleverer than me.

The other huge difference in pre-school education was that in England, all age groups, from 2-5, were catered for within the same space. I was used to teaching a group of children of the same age in a separate classroom, where we had desks and a semblance of orderliness. I was further astounded to know that the children could pretty much do what they wanted when they wanted. They could make choices.

I was expected to go down to a child's level when talking to them and not to call across a room if I wanted their attention. This was not African teaching. My language had to change. My tone had to change. I had to change. It was exhausting.

It took me just over two years to soften my teaching practice and learn new skills.

After a couple of years teaching at Circus Pre-school, I returned to the world of real estate.

After my time at Pam Golding Properties in Johannesburg I knew a little about property. Remax was a South African property company that had just made its debut over in the UK and a Brighton branch was formed. An English couple ran the Remax branch. They got together an eclectic bunch of wanna-be estate agents to train and hopefully make them rich. We were like characters from a comedy sit-com. Most of us were from either South Africa, Zimbabwe or from another outpost. Barely British, we knew nothing about the way buying or selling property worked in this country. I passed the Remax exam with 100% and still knew nothing.

Anyway, I showed properties and took offers and processed paperwork and made a little bit to keep home and hearth going. As this job was commission only I also acted as a supply teacher to cover any financial gaps.

However, income was not consistent neither was the call for supply teaching. Life was getting rough and it would get rougher still.

It was that this point our working visas expired and we were refused Indefinite Leave to Remain.

Our application was denied after four years of living in the United Kingdom. This was based on the fact I had accessed Working Tax Credits for two years thereby unknowingly defrauding the Government. This was a surprise for me as I had been advised to apply by a community leader and had filled in the application honestly. Working Tax Credits were new and there was confusion by all and sundry as to whether it was a considered a benefit or not.

I spent months compiling papers to prove the children and I were not illegal aliens but eligible to stay. Our first appeal was also unsuccessful so working with an immigration lawyer, I prepared for court.

The court had the final say in our future and our lawyer was not hopeful in the slightest. The outcome of the trial was sent by post a week after and if found guilty of using public funds illegally we would be expected to leave the country within twenty-eight days.

Leaving Heather at home with friends, Richard and James accompanied me to the court in London. We had nothing going for us except who we were and what we looked like. We scrubbed up well, boys suited and booted and me in a smart-casual outfit that screamed respectability. If the only thing we had was looking good then we'd look very good.

Entering the court building we were surrounded by hundreds of other foreigners attending court hoping to stop their deportation. The smell of anxiety and desperation hung heavy in the air and made me feel hopeless.

Our names were called and we were ushered into the small court room. It was then we were told that we would stand before the only blind judge of the circuit. Terrific. All we had was looking good! Events took on a surreal quality when the judge stopped the prosecutor from speaking and said he wanted to hear from me. I stood up and told him our story.

In closing, the judge said he was not going to make us wait for his ruling. In fact, he wanted to tell us right then and there that he was going to allow us to stay. The boys and I stepped outside the court room and burst into tears.

We held a Legal Aliens party at home the following week, celebrating with thirty of our friends, drinking bubbly and eating fish and chips wrapped in newspaper with mushy peas on the side.

Work and whimsy

In July 2007 I moved from my ex-Council house in Hangleton to a flat nearby. Situated in Court Farm Road, the three-storey brick and hung tile vernacular revival flats had sloping tiled roofs with dormers and surrounded a central green. It was my first home after the divorce, my place of peace. Richard lived in digs in university in Kingston-upon-Thames and James moved into his first home, a rented studio flat near Hove station. So Heather and I made our flat into our little home.

I had just about enough furniture to kit out my flat but did not have a sofa, only two deck chairs to use for watching telly. On moving day I hired a big white van and our church friends helped us move. After a few trips we were pretty much done although I did side-swipe a few cars in the gardens of our new abode when I drove the van. Then, on a return trip to check on the old house we drove past a house that had a beautiful brown leather sofa sitting outside their fence. We knocked on the door, checked if it was free to collect, then loaded it into the back of the van and took it to Court Farm Road. It was nearly brand new and it fitted in my lounge like it was made to measure. It was the perfect house-warming present.

Soon after we settled in, I got a phone call as I was walking to the nearby shops. It was Carrie, my friend from Johannesburg. As with my friend Jill, we had gone to the same church, our children went to pre-school together and we had shared many laughs and tears during our friendship. I connected with her because she was mad as a box of frogs and often quite unpredictable.

Jill, Carrie and I formed a triad. We were like the witches of Eastwick and just as crazy. In Johannesburg, all three of us were patients of the long-suffering Dr Patrick McGraw, the psychiatrist who helped me through my break-down. Now, all three of us were in the UK together and still clearly in need of Dr McGraw's skills.

Carrie's whimsical unpredictability was evident in her phone call. She had had sold her home, decided to come to the UK as a carer and was leaving in a few days time.

Carrie arrived within the week and we became a blended family. Carrie, Heather and I curled up on the precious leather sofa every night like a heap of lazy cats, watched television and ate lots of chocolate.

Heather's school, Blatchington Mill High School, was a block away so she became a latch-key kid when she started high school in the September. One of my key memories of that school year was when Heather had to do a project for Biology. Her task was to make a model of any kind of cell structure and she chose to make a sperm cell. She blew up a large balloon in our kitchen and covered it with paper mache. She tweaked the shape, giving it a bit of a personality, then painted it with what she hoped was sperm colour. She trotted off to school the next day proudly carrying this enormous sperm under her arm. It was the one project for which she got very good marks.

Heather and I lived in this flat for just over a year before being evicted. Living below our flat was an extremely crotchety old man and his wife, who suffered from dementia. He was the scourge of the estate and constantly told off his neighbours for doing nothing but breathing. He came raging up to our flat whenever he felt we were making too much noise whilst doing horrendous activities like eating, sleeping, or watching telly. One time he bashed at our door because he could hear our visitor's baby crawling across the floor. This cowardly ray of sunshine also became verbally and racially abusive to Heather when she entered the flat after school or when I was otherwise occupied.

Unfortunately he was pals with the equally grumpy old soul who managed the estate so any concerns I took to him were ignored. The complaints against us kept on mounting and between the two of them, they managed to ensure that my lease was not extended after a year. Naturally I fought this decision and stayed on in the flat until an eviction notice came. I now had the task of finding another place to rent at an affordable price near Heather's school.

Rentals are extraordinarily high in Brighton & Hove. At the time I earned £1,100 per month and the average monthly rental for a two-bedroom flat was £900. Without child benefit payments and working tax credits I could not survive. Besides which, just finding a reasonable property was very difficult. The best possible one I could find was a very dark and poky flat above a shop overlooking a supermarket car park. Just as I was about to sign up for it, we saw a three-bedroom maisonette in Hangleton Road on offer for £750 per month.

I nabbed my friend Colleen and charged around to view the flat with Heather in tow. I chose Colleen because she was canny and wise. Over seventy years old, a stalwart Christian, she knew about life and she knew what I needed. She was my mentor and I could rely on her. Unfortunately, I was not as good for her as she was for me. I had introduced Colleen to Pimms on one of her birthdays and we try to keep a birthday Pimms as part of our summer tradition. The first time she savoured this heavenly goblet of sunshine was in a little café in George Street. She found it quite delightful and drank it with relish. It went straight to her legs. We left the café and she tottered up the street, listing at an angle. 'I can't feel my shlegs!' she giggled as she tried her hardest to straighten her course. I figured that as our latest birthday Pimms had been drunk about a month beforehand, she was in a reasonable state of mind to offer wise counsel. We concurred it was just the thing so Heather and I became its latest tenants within the month.

As we settled in, I realized that I needed someone else to love. Someone who, unlike Heather, would not answer me back or constantly demand my time and my hard-earned cash. So I got a kitty.

Richard's sister-in-law, who lived in Scotland, had a cat that had just given birth to kittens. I wanted one of those. So this chosen feline was transported to Liverpool to stay with Alan's parents for a few days, after which Alan collected him and drove him down to London. The next day I drove out of Brighton during rush hour to fetch our new kitty. We spent a half hour there then brought kitty back to his new home. It was a mammoth trip for a tiny creature just leaving his mum. We had to find a name for him and Heather suggested we call him TopDeck after a South African chocolate bar of the same name. This chocolate bar had two layers, the bottom one was brown milk chocolate and the top was white milky bar chocolate – just like me and you she said. So TopDeck he remained.

He really did fill an emotional gap and in fact, he still does. He is my fourth child, my fur ball of joy, my stress-reliever and my hot-water bottle, even in the summer.

* * *

Whilst I waited for my visa issues to be resolved I was not allowed to teach so had to try other types of employment. I linked up with an employment agency although my skill set was limited. I could teach and I could draw naked people well and I could rent houses to people in South Africa but really I was of no earthly good in the English working world. An architectural company based in Brighton needed a receptionist/administrator to cover for two weeks and I was taken on. I ended up staying for two and a half years, mainly because it's quite hard to give staff the sack these days. I didn't know anything. I had no idea what toner was or how to replace a cartridge, I couldn't use Outlook, ordering of office supplies was bewildering – who knew you could get three hundred different types of staplers? – and filing was a mystery. However, I could answer the phone most professionally and make tea really well.

The office manager, Mandy, had all the architects and bosses around her little finger. She was the heart of the business and made it run smoothly and efficiently. The other administrator was Laura, a stunning Northern girl with skin like alabaster and hair the colour of the setting sun. Laura showed me how computer programmes worked and helped me endlessly with other tasks I didn't understand. I used to feel quite intelligent until I worked as an administrator. Now, the only thing I could do with confidence was open the mail and record the post in the post book.

It didn't help that my eyes had started to fail and despite wearing glasses I could not see words on the computer screen unless I used giant font. Mandy even got me a magnifying glass to help me read business cards. If written text was grey I couldn't see the words at all

There were too many cringe-worthy events of mishap and failure to relate but after I tried inserting a bottle of powder black toner only to misjudge and have it explode all over the office I knew my time was up. I was not cut out to be an office worker. The relief from my bosses was tangible.

The world continued to blur. I couldn't recognise close friends from a few paces away and spent a couple of years waving happily at some very confused people I had never met. Driving was an adventure for me and a nightmare for other drivers. I couldn't see where kerbs started nor could I read road signs. Heather, who was about twelve at the time, was my navigator. Her screams usually did the trick in telling me I was veering off road or about to crash into pedestrians but that was not an altogether foolproof technique. When the weather was foggy all hope was lost.

At my last optician appointment I had been told that my eyeballs had lost their elasticity. Super. So had my breasts, my jowls and the skin covering my knees. He made me do an eye test that showed how far you could see in all directions. I had to push a buzzer every time a little dot appeared on the screen. After several attempts I burst into tears and sobbed 'I can't see any stupid dots!' in my optician's face (I think it was his face, I couldn't really see). Unsurprisingly, he advised me I had cataracts.

Going to the eye hospital made me feel like a spring chicken, as the average age was about eighty years old. Much to my shame though, I was not half as brave as other patients. I can't even let someone else put on my mascara, never mind take hold of my eyelids and prise them apart. I was noted as being 'a nervous patient' and could then have general anaesethic, unlike the older brave-hearts who had a good old chin-wag with the surgeon whilst their corneas were being peeled.

There is something about being put to sleep that is quite lovely. I do wish it was legal to have a drip attached to my bed where I could plug in every night and have sleep pumped straight into my body.

Taking off the eye patches a day after the operations was an experience of Biblical proportions. I could see! I saw signs and notices and buildings and numbers and people's faces and cars and clouds, as clear and bright as sunshine. I saw people's pores! Some people I knew had freckles! I could read business cards and telephone numbers and newspapers. My biggest shock was looking at myself in the mirror. No longer was I in soft focus and I saw every line, chin hair, blemish, broken vein and wrinkle. It was brutal.

A few months later I had to go back to have each eye lasered. This process was even worse than the operations because I had to be awake. The nice doctor first put stinging yellow eye drops in my screwed up eyes. I wept yellow tears through slitty eyes, like a very unhappy jaundiced lizard until I was numb and glassy-eyed enough to have the lasering done.

The eye doctor looked like she was about thirteen and I had to have a sudden leap of faith to allow a teenager anywhere near my eyeballs. Once she had clamped my head into a vice she had me where she wanted me and barked instructions at me as if I was a kid. All I was doing was whining and pouting and whimpering so she really had no right to be so stroppy. She told me to keep my eyes open so she could place a lens contraption ONTO MY EYEBALL. Using her fingers like pincers, she pulled my lids apart and put this object onto my eye. I clamped my eyes shut so tightly it shot out straight back at her. She kept on telling me to open my eyes – I was convinced they were open – and when she finally won the battle I sat imprisoned in the vice, staring malevolently at her through my one lens-free eye while she tasered, I mean, lasered the other one.

* * *

After the toner incident and many other misdemeanours at the architect's practice I decided to return to Early Years education. Fortuitously, I was appointed as the manager of a pre-school in Hove the week after I resigned.

I only got the job because they were desperate. Emma, chair of the committee, had one week in which to find a manager or the pre-school would close. There had been a succession of staff and managers, including one manager who preferred to drink in the cupboard rather than face the children every day. It was make or break time and as school was starting again so soon, I had to do.

The pre-school used a church hall as their venue. At the back was a narrow cupboard running half the width of the hall and this housed all the equipment and resources of the pre-school. Every morning and every afternoon the entire school had to be put out then re-packed. I should have worked for Pickfords. My biceps trebled in size over the next four years. No wonder one of the managers had turned to drink.

The church hall sat next to the main church off a main road. A graveyard surrounded the church and abutted the hall's play area. There was lots of fun to be had during rat season as the rats, the size of wild cats, stuck their heads out from beneath the gravestones and ran hell-for-leather across the path into the Wendy house. We had a mice infestation once and had to close the school to sterilise all the equipment. Scrubbing boxes upon boxes of Lego and stickle bricks and other bitty resources with toothbrushes dipped in anti-bac is not a barrel of laughs.

Another thing we had to contend with was passing trade and local graveyard inhabitants. As we were situated on a busy road near an unusually diverse shopping area, we often got interrupted by the lost, the lonely and the downright loony. The graveyard inhabitants comprised homeless folk who met to drink together in the shade of the trees and shoot the breeze. It became a problem when they decided to use our back door as a toilet or they hung over the play area fence, swigging from their bottles.

Amidst all this, the pre-school thrived. It helped that most of the staff were hard-working and up for a laugh. One staff member, Liz, was the best practitioner I had ever had the privilege of working with and I learned so much just by watching her teach. She stood with me during my time of mourning for John and was also complicit in finding me my next husband in 2012.

John

I met John in late 2004, nearly two years after my divorce. I had dabbled in on-line dating and been astounded at the low level of life that emerged from the darkness of the web. The amount of men the world over who want to show off their appendages in technicolour is astonishing. They do this sometimes without even asking, which is even more impolite. I got tired of being asked what I was wearing. If only they knew. Fluffy slippers, old trackie-bottoms, a sleep T-shirt and a dressing gown that had seen better days was not what they were imagining. Even so, it was a seductive, if destructive, pastime for a newly divorced woman who needed to feel wanted and desired.

I went on a few dates which were eye-opening. The last dating experience I'd had was when I was nineteen. Gus and I spent some time together but despite our best efforts there was no romantic spark. He had a great sense of humour, held spiritual beliefs, was a father of two and a carer for his mum. However, he thought so little of himself he couldn't even accept a compliment. I didn't have the energy to continually boost his self-esteem and it seemed he was happier looking after his pond full of exotic koi and polishing his Harley Davidson which he kept parked in the kitchen.

The next man I dated for a couple of months was playboy Stephen. At fifty years old he was still finding out what he wanted to be when he was grown up. Although I fully understood that feeling, he most certainly wasn't a keeper. Besides which, he kissed very badly. He had an encyclopaedic knowledge of all the ways a bloke must not kiss a girl. He was like the Wide-Mouthed-Frog. Or the Chomp hippo. I got jaw-ache.

Then I received a message from John. He was clearly a cut above the rest. He wrote well, using punctuation and correct spelling. He was witty and clearly intelligent. He was a police officer serving in Brighton but lived in Littlehampton and he liked my profile. I liked his writing but didn't know what he looked like as he had not put a photo on his profile.

We corresponded by email for a couple of months before actually meeting. In my mind's eye I imagined him to look like a sea-faring captain, portly, jovial and with a rum-induced twinkle in his eye. Turns out he was thin and wiry and looked a lot like a younger Jack Straw, the Labour politician. We met at The Grenadier Pub, down the road from my house and clicked immediately.

John, a Northerner, was the master of brevity and hilarity. He could sum up a situation in three words or less. His minimalistic style translated into his home, a one-bedroom flat in the gorgeous village of Littlehampton on the Sussex coast. He had only what was necessary for life. His fridge had ice and milk and the occasional ready meal for one. He always made me tea when I arrived at his flat which he served with one digestive biscuit on a plate. At Christmas time he went the extra mile by putting two baubles on a mini-Christmas tree thirty centimetres high and by decorating his telly with one short piece of tinsel.

He loved his job as a police officer and recounted reams of stories of misadventure and criminal stupidity. I loved him but I also knew he was not the marrying kind and after my divorce, nor was I. So our relationship suited us both. He made me feel whole and happy and made me laugh again and I will always be grateful for the time we had together.

A year into our relationship John phoned me and told me to sit down whilst he spoke. Sitting down on the bed, I held the phone tightly. He said he had just been told he had terminal cancer. I knew he'd gone to the local hospital for tests as he was experiencing fierce night sweats and had been feeling run down but this news was totally unexpected.

It felt so unfair. John was fit, trim, he did not eat salt, he hardly drank alcohol at all and he didn't smoke. His cancer was genetic in origin and it attacked him with unremitting force.

For the next four years John battled the disease. He never lost his sense of humour or his brilliant mind. During his illness and in-between hospital stays he studied for the police Sergeants' exam and passed. He moved to be nearer Brighton and rented a cottage in Chailey, near Lewes. It was his last home. We spent time there just lying in each other's arms, talking about life and death, the past and the future. From there he moved to his brother's home in Norwich and then to a hospice to live out his final days. His brothers kindly paid for me to come up to his funeral and stay overnight in a hotel to make the trip from Brighton easier. Riding in the funeral cars with his family was a privilege I will never forget. A police guard of honour formed outside the chapel as his coffin, draped in police colours, was carried in.

John was one of a kind, a man amongst men and the world is poorer without him.

I turned fifty three months after John's death.

I celebrated my birthday by having a Pink Tie and Tiara evening at The Shelley's Hotel in Lewes where my fabulous friend Jana worked. The four star hotel, a 17th Century country house, had a charming olde worlde feel about it. My parents and my sister had flown out from South Africa and Australia respectively to celebrate with me and old friends from around the UK had also made the effort to come and party.

John's two brothers, whom I had met at his funeral, came as well. He had been very close to them and having them there was wonderful and sad at the same time. Saying goodbye to them after the party was the closing of yet another chapter of my life.

Alan, Farewell

The day I was told John had died, was the day I learned that Alan had only a few months left to live.

Alan phoned me on a Sunday as I was leaving church and asked me to visit him in hospital. I had no idea he'd been that ill so it was a bit of a shock. James, Heather and I drove up to the County Hospital and found Alan in a surgical ward, looking very thin and feeble. His smile lit up the room when he saw us. The doctor came through and explained quite bluntly that Alan had colon cancer and there was no cure and no effective treatment. This was terminal. The only thing they would do was give him a colostomy bag which would prolong life by a few months.

The operation was performed the next day and after a few days, Alan moved back to his room at the Ship Hotel, on the Brighton beachfront. He had been working as a valet and car park attendant and had a bedroom in staff quarters. It quickly became quite obvious that he couldn't take care of himself in that room so the hotel very kindly gave him a top-floor suite in which he could rest and recuperate. Meals were brought to him and staff checked on him during the day to see if he was okay.

Heather and I visited often. She made him cry with laughter as she pulled her trademark 'bunny faces' at him and told him jokes. My parents had come to visit from South Africa for my fiftieth birthday and we spent some time with him together. One day we all took him for an outing, pushing him in a wheelchair along the promenade to the pier. He was too weak to spend too much time outdoors and in a great deal of pain but he was so pleased to be with us. We sat in the plush hotel lounge and chatted about everything and nothing, just 'being.'

A few months later Alan became weaker and I took him to hospital again. It was then that Richard came out to his father. With some deep trepidation, he introduced him to his Alan, his boyfriend and future husband. There was no need to fear, Alan listened and nodded and smiled and told me later that they had his blessing. Thereafter, he lay silent most of the time, sipping water and listening to us talk as we sat beside him. Soon, the day came when the doctors suggested it was time for him to go to a hospice.

The hospice was in Peacehaven, just outside Brighton and near the top of the chalk cliffs which cut down into the sea. No staff members wore uniforms and the place was run as a home rather than a medical facility. Alan was put into a room containing a hospital-type bed, chest of drawers and armchairs. We put photos on the dressing table and tried to make it look homely. We visited every day for three days, bringing him his favourite food treats he could not eat and telling him news he could hardly hear.

On the fourth day, staff told us he was losing the fight and getting ready to go. Richard came down from university and we all went to see him. He knew we were all there with him, a family reunited at this final transition.

Witnessing a loved one moving from life to death is an indescribably heart-wrenching process. Alan's breaths became more ragged and his skin started losing colour. His heart beat slowed so much his pulse was very difficult to find. He took extended gaps between breaths and I waited, anguished, to hear his next breath. Just then, I felt Alan's mother there, so close, just on the other side of this life. She was waiting and she was filled with joy, ready to welcome him home.

Alan sighed his last breath and I could almost see him leaving his earthly body and rising into eternity. He was at peace.

Collecting his ashes from the funeral parlour was difficult for us to process. James and I drove to Peacehaven and fetched them. The ashes were sealed within a green, paisley-patterned box which James held with great care as we travelled home. He still sits on my bookshelf in the lounge. One day, when the time is right, we will place him in a beautiful forest clearing, close to the nature he loved.

Disney Dash

A week after Alan died, Rich and Alan took James, Heather and I to Disneyworld in Florida. They had both gone there before and loved the experience. We flew out to New York in-between blizzards in London and ended up being diverted to Chicago as blizzards had cut off that airport too. It was a long trip. We were like the walking dead when we arrived in Chicago after midnight and had to queue up for a room at the hotel with over a hundred other passengers. As Alan and Rich sorted out arrangements the three of us slumped into lounge chairs, heads back, eyes closed, open-mouthed. There was snoring and drooling involved. Rich later said that pointing us out to the booking manager was one of the proudest moments of his life. I assume he was being sarcastic.

So our first night of sleeping on American soil was in the Chicago Hyatt Hotel. Actually it was only part of a night and breakfast came far too soon. We got a connecting flight to Miami later that day.

We stayed in a villa within a gated community and drove a huge hire car to and from attractions. Living altogether was interesting. As an Aspie, James struggled to cope with everyone living in such close quarters; Heather was an undiagnosed ADHD teenager (say no more), I was somewhat overcome by life after a year of loss and Rich and Alan were the Sergeant Majors as well as our personal stylists.

We had to look good every day. We could no longer wear our trailer trash gear, we had to Hollister up. I know nothing about image but mistakes were made. The worst one was when Alan gave me a haircut. My hair is naturally frizzy and in this Southern heat it bushed out beautifully. What possessed him I do not know, but he gave me a bob. A bob on a chubster is not a good look. Add extra crinkle and you are talking disaster. He didn't even have the decency to hide his horrified giggle once he was finished shearing.

The holiday was like a boot camp with Rich and Alan as the Sergeant Majors. Up by 7:00! Shower and dress by 7:30! Breakfast at 7:30! Clean teeth at 7:38! Grab bags and sunglasses and exit the villa by 7:42! Climb into the mean machine, click door locks at 7:45!

Roaring off down the motorway we played Lady Gaga at full bore and sang 'we were born this way!' at the top of our lungs.

We did the daily Disney-Dash. To get into Disneyworld, we had to park the car miles away in a Disney car park and then catch a Disney train to the actual entrance. The boys wanted to avoid the queues for rides so as we screeched to a halt in the car park we threw ourselves bodily out the car and obeyed the yelled instruction – 'RUN!'

I was fifty and fat. What I did as 'running' was very different to the accepted dictionary definition. I bobbled along, arms swinging hard from side to side to get momentum, my gaze focussed on the prize – a disappearing train. Breathless, I'd meet the rest of them at the train gate and try to ignore the eye-rolling. I treasured the train ride because as soon as it stopped, the Sergeant Majors barked the 'RUN!' command and we had to leap off and run furiously towards the entrance of Disneyworld.

I was exhausted before I even got into the land of castles and fairies and terrifying rides. However, the running didn't stop as we had to get to the most popular rides before eight thousand other runners got there. It was like the straggle end of the London Marathon.

I discovered that Rich and Alan were wicked liars and had no respect for older women at all. This ride is fine, they'd say, nothing to worry about! No, mum, it doesn't flip over and do cartwheels whilst you're in it. Nah, this does not shoot you into the air at warp speed and make your face fat shake uncontrollably. Ah, this one is nice – it's just a water ride – you certainly will not scream as you thunder down a mile-high tube. And as for the Everest ride, what a joy!

I spent most of our stay at the Disney resorts screaming but my undoing was the Everest ride. The boys helpfully supported me as I climbed into a little wooden box cart and held onto a rail in front of my seat. There were about eight people in each cart and everyone looked really excited. We chugged out onto a rail with a mountain ahead of us and faux-Himalayan scenery all around. It was pleasant. We got to the first little rise and I panicked a bit. We got to the second rise which was almost vertical and I panicked a lot.

The little wooden box cart shot up a rail track into thin air. I got vertigo at the best of times and this sent me doolally. There was nothing but air as we shot ever upwards towards the peak of the mountain. I was too terrified to scream; too scared to keep my eyes open and too scared to keep them closed. The train gathered even more speed and shot through the mountain into nothingness. Ahead were broken twisted train tracks, their track ends pointing upwards as if in beseeching prayer.

The train shuddered to a shrieking halt at the broken end. The only way onwards was a downward death dive. Oh no it wasn't! Of course, we had to reverse at full speed and hurtle backwards down the same route which was ten times worse than doing it the right way round.

I had to be helped from the box cart when the ride finished and limped sobbing past people still queuing up to do the ride. Rich and Alan tried to be comforting but being comforting was terribly hard as they couldn't even see through their tears of laughter.

We met Mickey Mouse, lots of princesses and Spiderman. We ate turkey drumsticks which were the size of dinosaur legs and promptly became violently ill. We watched the Disney night-time parade in front of a lit-up Disney castle. We visited every park and tourist trap in the whole vicinity, even taking time to see manatees at a manatee park and drive to Daytona Beach.

Going out to eat in Florida was quite an experience. I was astonished at the portion sizes offered. Steaks were like platters and puddings were big enough to cause instant onset of diabetes. Breakfasting at a diner, we watched as hugely obese families helped themselves to grits, eggs, porridge, chips, éclairs, mini gateaux, toast, bacon, pancakes and maple syrup all on one plate. And that was just the first helping. Besides feeling awfully skinny next to this lot, I also felt very virtuous as my plate was not quite so full.

As a good parent, one hopes for the best for your children. You are their protector and you would lay down your life to keep them safe. You wouldn't insist they be shot up into the air whilst sat in a slingshot and cry with mirth at the utter fear showing in their popping-out eyes.

It really was the funniest thing I've ever seen. Richard persuaded Heather to ride The Slingshot with him. This contraption encased the rider in a seat then shot them heavenward at a hundred miles an hour. The slingshot would bounce back and forth between this world and the next until it came to a stop. Heather and Rich sat together in the two-seater slingshot waiting for lift-off. Heather was so scared she could hardly speak except to stutter she wanted to get off. We all watched, trying our hardest not to laugh, as she begged Rich not to do this to her. Rich couldn't stop chuckling. Eventually the operator thought enough was enough and he let it rip.

Watching the video of this ride is side-splitting. Richard laughs like a drain at Heather all ride long while she cries and laughs and screams that she's going to die all at the same time.

I am probably not a very good parent. I put the video on YouTube and play it from time to time when I need cheering up.

https://www.youtube.com/watch?v=lLAsZMnVpe8

Richard and Alan - Wedding

Rich proposed to Alan at Edinburgh Castle and he happily accepted. It was just before marriage between same-sex couples was made legal so they arranged a civil ceremony service in London, near where they lived.

Naturally, all the family had to be styled by the betrothed couple so we would bring honour to the Bebb name. As it was a gay wedding, there was no limit to sparkle, feathers and froufrou. I bought the most gorgeous pair of high-heeled silver shoes and the boys chose a Julian MacDonald frock and a purple fascinator for me to wear. They chose a hot little leopard-skin number for Heather and suited and booted James.

The boys booked us into the local Travel Lodge for the wedding and Carrie joined us there to get ready. Exceedingly unsteady on my feet, I tottered down the street to the venue, clutching onto James in order to stay upright.

The ceremony was held in a charming old chapel in Kingston-upon-Thames. Richard and Alan looked devastatingly handsome in their kilts and formal Scottish wear. Heather, face like thunder as she thought she was losing her brother forever, marched down the aisle in towering stilettos, throwing rose petals in the aisle before the boys came in. She then sat in the front row and sobbed through the service.

It was a beautiful ceremony. Love shone through like sun through stained glass as they exchanged vows and shared their commitment with us. Then it was party time!

Partying with a bunch of predominately gay Scotsmen and women is the ultimate night out. The girls danced reels in heels as the men flew around the room with kilts and sporrans a-flapping to the Celtic beat.

Having eaten a seven-course Italian dinner we needed to work some of that off and highland-flinging used up thousands of calories.

In the wee hours, we traipsed back to our hotel with shoes in one hand and flip-flops on our feet. It had been quite a night.

Rich and Riches

Since becoming a single mother of three children the struggle to survive financially had been one of fear and faith, usually not in equal measure. This thread of money worries wove itself through every aspect of my life in the first years of my stay in Brighton. For the first couple of years after we separated Alan was not able to contribute as he was living under the radar as an illegal resident. He had not extended his visa after our divorce so his job had to end.

Rent was expensive, utility payments kept on increasing and kids had to fed and clothed on a low salary. Family and friends helped as much as they could but there was always more month than money. As the years passed I began running out of options.

Bills came by the bag, most of them with a red arrow on the envelope pointing accusingly at the words 'Final Demand!' printed in bold on the envelope. Phone calls requesting payments rang in even at night time and the pressure began to build.

After years of juggling I had exhausted credit cards, bank overdrafts and loans. I couldn't even pray or think about it all. I just tried to block it all out by ignoring envelopes and unplugging the phone. The sound of the post box flap snapping when post was delivered made my heart race. It was never good news.

I felt like a complete failure. Here I was, an intelligent, well-spoken, educated woman (I thought!) who couldn't pay her bills and support her family. Even though I worked as hard as I could, I could not cope. It's a difficult thing to share with anyone – I discovered that dealing with debt is an extremely lonely, depressing and isolating existence.

Then, as I was losing all hope, along came a very strange angel indeed. I had met an angel dressed in a safari suit before and now I was to meet one who had an unearthly passion of fixing other people's money problems. This heaven-sent being was called Rich, which I thought was a very promising start to my problems. Rich had set up a branch of Christians Against Poverty (CAP), a debt-relief agency, at the church I attended and I was his very first client. Lucky him.

He suffered stoically through my first sobbing chat with him and calmly started the long process of sorting me and my finances out. I gave him a pile of unopened bills and letters of demand, invoices and other paperwork related to my fiscal fiasco and he took care of them. I didn't open a bill for two years. Rich became my debt coach and liaised with my banks, debtors and utility companies. He put together a plan to pay all my debts off and slowly but surely I began to feel in control once more. After a couple of years my income dropped due to a salary cut and a benefit cessation and my debt plan had to change. The only option left open to me to repay remaining debt was to apply for a Debt Relief Order and even this was all done for me by Rich and CAP, efficiently and in double quick time.

At last, I became debt free. I lost the stress along with my creditors and I gained a friend for life in Rich.

The Climb

I thought it may be a brilliant idea to do something out of the ordinary to raise funds for St Andrew's Community Pre-school which I was managing. A few of us would climb Mt Snowdon and raise money through sponsorship. I realised a little training was called for.

My mind was in the right place for exercise for once. This was a highly unusual state for me as I am not a gym bunny at the best of times. However, a few months before this idea took hold I had started a Running for Beginners training programme. It was an interval training programme which meant I could walk then run then walk, adjusting times as I went along.

The first task was to walk for three minutes and run for one. Even though I had my Nikes on I was clueless as to how to actually run. My efforts at Disney were deplorable and I had not run since. It's amazing how scary it is to lift one foot up and then another and move forward simultaneously. How do I get momentum going? I wondered. Somehow I began doing the shuffling jog, stealing glances at my timer to see how fast one minute was. One minute was forever, I discovered. I got the hang of it over time but it was never a pretty sight. I was so self-conscious I only did this programme after night had fallen and Hove Park was deserted.

My friend Pam, a South African woman who was managing the The Ark Pre-school at the time, decided to join us in this venture. So together we set up a training schedule of hill-walking along the Downs, a very hilly area close to our homes. Rain or shine, we marched up and down the hills for at least once a week for three months and I felt really fit at the end of it all.

Not fit enough, sadly. Climbing Mt Snowdon was heavy going. Starting the hike with my group, I walked up a particularly steep slope after about 600 metres of gentle rise and breathlessly wondered how much further we had to go. Just then I saw a sign that said Start of Route. The start? Despondency set in but it was do or die, so I did, and felt like I was dying. Halfway up there is a small building with toilets and an area in which you can stand around and drink some water. The walls were adorned with newspaper articles about the perils of climbing Mt Snowdon and stories about fatalities that had occurred over the years. It was not a cheering read.

My fellow hikers helped me by carrying my backpack and by slowing their pace. I was the oldest member of the group and they showed me and my advanced age great respect. However I realised age was not a factor in fitness as various elderly wrinklies strode past me at regular intervals. One Japanese woman, who was eighty at the very least, skipped past me like a mountain bunny and disappeared over the next rise, kicking up dust as she went.

I used my camera as a tool to breathe. The scenery was beautiful and vistas changed around every corner, making Kodak moments frequent. I'd climb for ten minutes, announce it was Kodak moment time then take photos until I could breathe again. Little by little we made it. We reached the summit and posed for the obligatory photo. I phoned Mike from atop Mt Snowdon, ecstatic to be at the top of the world.

What goes up must come down. The hike down the mountain was abominable. My knees gave in and the pain was agonizing. Near the bottom of the mountain my toes started to hurt terribly so I sat down and took off my hiking boots. My big toes were a bloodied mess, the toenails tearing off and lifting up from my flesh. I hobbled wretchedly the rest of the way down. Walking for days afterwards was absolutely hideous. Every joint in my body rebelled. I was the walking wounded. But I did it!

Broken Bride

During Heather's high school years I usually sent her to South Africa for the summer holidays. This was for two reasons. Firstly, I was working from 8:00-5:30pm every day and child care was prohibitively expensive. It was cheaper to fly her to my mother's home than to book her into all-day clubs. Secondly, I needed the break. After the sperm modelling high, Heather's high school grades had dipped drastically due to her off-the-wall behaviour. She was high maintenance.

She became a seasoned traveller and flying long-haul alone didn't worry her too much at all. One time, on the day she was due to fly, I set out her suitcase and ticket and passport. Idly flicking through her passport I froze, mid-flick. Her passport was out of date! I gabbled down the phone to the airline, paid extra for her to fly in three days time and phoned my parents to say she wouldn't be arriving until later. The next day we went up to London and got a one-page exit letter allowing her to fly without a passport. Kathy, Jenny's daughter, helped her get another passport whilst she was there so she could return. There always seemed to be drama in my world and this oversight was most certainly a drama of my own making.

Even after her heart bypass my mother still suffered from heart disease and during the past few years her angina had really played up. She'd phone me in the darkest hours when she was having an attack. My dad was deaf so he couldn't hear her from his room so she'd call me, thousands of miles away in a different hemisphere. If I heard heavy breathing when I answered the phone at night I knew it wasn't the local sex-pest nut-job, it was my mother gasping as her heart squeezed.

I talked her through every attack, helpfully instructing her to breathe, as if she had no notion that was what she had to do. After she took her pills her chest pains eased and she thanked me, telling me to sleep tight and not to worry. That was unlikely. I spent the next hour after these episodes with my eyes bulging with anxiety and my heart racing uncomfortably.

My mother was a danger to herself too. She used a mobility scooter to scoot around the retirement village, going to her bridge games and the dining hall and the main office to collect post. On one unforgettable morning she clambered on her scooter which was parked by her front door and opened the throttle. To her horror she rode over her own foot. It was such a shock she reversed, riding over it once more. This was so traumatising she accelerated and promptly rode over her foot for the third time. Her foot turned blue and swelled up like a blowfish. I could not stop laughing even though she had to keep her foot raised and rested for weeks afterwards.

This reminded me of the time my mother met my brother David's first wife's family. They lived in the country and we travelled up to meet his wife's mother and other family members. It was stinking hot and we dressed very simply in dresses and sandals. David's mother-in-law leant towards my mother, touched her arm and said how much she loved the beautiful bluey-mauve stockings my mother was wearing. Such an unusual shade! My mother stared at her in disbelief. I am not *wearing* any stockings, she said through gritted teeth, tucking her varicose-veined legs under the chair.

One summer holiday trip coincided with the death of my mother.

On arrival at the airport, Heather was collected by Kathy, who took Heather straight to the Olivedale Clinic to visit granny, who was there as a precautionary measure as she was feeling a bit more unwell than usual. My mother was so happy to see them. Heather adored her granny and couldn't wait to spend the holiday with her once she was back at home. After spending some time together, Kathy and Heather left.

Back in England, I received a phone call at home mid-morning. I was expecting this as a confirmation call that Heather had landed safely. It was Kathy. She told me, through many tears, that my mother died an hour after seeing them. Just like that. Her heart finally broke, gave up the fight and she went home. I screamed down the phone, hardly able to believe she had gone, my heart feeling like it had splintered into a million pieces.

I couldn't go to her funeral for financial reasons. My brave Heather stood in for me at that time, with help and support from Kathy. Her passing left a crater in the lives of her family. I have yet to mourn her properly, if there is such a thing. How can someone of such substance disappear from life and never return?

Not many people know that my mother already had a broken heart from when she was in her first years of infant school. The one person she should have trusted in this life, her father, broke her body and her spirit until she was thirteen years old. He brutally raped her throughout these years, at times leaving her unable to walk. She spent all her life trying to find release from her memories and to eradicate the nightmares of her soul. She married her handsome suitor when she was sixteen, needing to be mended, looked after, adored and cherished. She came to realise that no one person can heal such brokenness. To counteract her demons, she loved her family excessively, fiercely, overpoweringly. She was forever bruised, but she was a survivor.

I wrote her a simple poem, which I gave to her when she'd felt very ill a few months before her death. She'd found it a great comfort so Kathy read it out at her funeral.

Broken Bride

little girl of sorrows
spirit-torn, so raw
haunted eyes cloaked pain
no-one ever saw

gossamer child-bride
heard her groom say
darling, I'll love you forever
and take you far, far away

all through life's ages
this fragile girl grew
became a woman of substance
to all that she knew

hair a swathe of silver
honour for her years
her life a jewelled necklace
strung with secret tears

content now in spirit
yet weary in soul
her Bridegroom comes
to take His bride home

wiping her tears
He kisses her face
dresses her in pearls
and snow-white lace

carries her over the threshold
leads her to Heaven's shore
she smiles, radiant,
broken no more

Back in the United Kingdom, Richard and I went to Rottingdean, under the white chalk cliffs on the coast, to lay roses in the sea to mark her leaving. We wrote her name on the concrete walls supporting the cliffs using broken pieces of chalk that had crumbled from the cliff side and blew kisses into the shore wind.

I still think she will appear one day, visiting from South Africa and that I will help heave her up the stairs to my lounge and plonk her on the sofa. I'll make her weak coffee with loads of milk and we'll chat and laugh together until the tears run from her eyes and she loses all control of her bladder.

We shall go for an English tea to Steyning Tea Rooms and return to Sheffield Park Gardens, this time in the autumn, so she can be delighted by the brilliant autumn colours the park displays. I will take her on the bus to town, one of her favourite activities when visiting me, so she can people-watch and make friends with complete strangers within a twenty minute ride.

Above all, I will tell her just how much I love her.

Mike

If my future second husband had gone to a traditional marriage agency it would have gone something like this.

Good morning Sir! Welcome to the GERiatric Marriage Service, GERMS for short. How can I help you?

I'd like to find Mrs McFarlane the Third please, without having to search on the Internet. I've tried that and it's amazing how much trouble one can get into with just one click.

Of course! Happy to help. I'll need some details to make a match so let's have a look at your requirements. We'll begin with appearance. Age is assumed as we at GERMS specialize in the sphere of advanced-age love.

Okay, well, a bountiful figure is good. Squishy. Generous bosoms with an independent life and preferably well into their journey south. I am also fond of disappearing eyebrows.

Good choice Sir! Anything else?

Ah, yes indeed. Must have a good growth of under-chin hair. An extra dose of testosterone doesn't go amiss at our age, no? (chortle)

Quite. Moving on, how about the area of the mind? Any must-haves there?

Absolutely. Must be on antidepressants and have a history of mental health adventures. I like off-the-wall thinking.

Please understand why I have to ask this next question, Sir. In this day and age we have to tick many diversity boxes in order to acquire our funding. Please answer as honestly as you can. What cultural or ethnic background do you prefer?

Ah, that's easy. I'd like a foreign immigrant, one from a former Colony, if you don't mind.

Noted. What about children, Sir? Extended family?

Hmph. I dislike children intensely. However, I have three of my own and I do actually like them. Presumably my match will not have small children so yes, children are not a deal breaker.

And in keeping with the diversity theme, please could the following attributes be reflected in her children? My life has been somewhat limited in terms of diversity and inclusion – I am merely an elderly White African male, after all is said and done.

I understand fully, Sir. What particular diversities would you like to embrace in your future step-children?

You need to know I am a socially well-rounded gentleman but due simply to lack of opportunity there are still three areas about which I need to learn more. It's a short but complex list and it's highly doubtful you will find me a family who has all three.

You'd be surprised Sir! GERMS prides itself on finding the perfect match!

Okay, well, here goes. I want a gay step-child, a Black step-child with ADHD and a step-child with Aspergers.

Right-eo. I see what you mean, Sir. Let's park that one for the moment. Any other requirements before I begin my match-making?

Actually yes, there are. I'm very attracted towards a rehabilitated bankrupt. Also, I am a smoker and I need a non-smoker in my life to wave the air-freshener can in my direction every once in a while. Lastly, and this is important, I want an epic snorer, someone able to complement my own nocturnal monologues.

Thank you, Sir. This gives me a good idea of your wants and needs. Please excuse me whilst I lie down in a dark room for a while. I'll be back later to go through our listed ladies and find one who may be suitable.

(Later) Sir! Blow me down with a feather! I have a perfect match! There is only one proviso...

Splendid! What's the proviso?

It's like this, Sir. She prefers to meet men in a public convenience. Would that be a problem for you Sir?

* * *

It had been a Black Wednesday at work in October 2012. Liz and I had left St Andrew's Pre-school after a hectic day of teaching overactive knee-highs and popped up George Street to a new coffee shop for lunch.

I went up to the loo, relishing the fact I was sitting down away from children. Suddenly the door handle started turning frantically and it was clear there was a desperate person trying to get in. Taking my time, I completed my ablutions and opened the door, finding a handsome, silver-haired man lurking right outside. I scolded him for being so impatient and he responded with some witticism. Realising he had a South African accent I started asking him where he was from. He wasn't too forthcoming as he only had one thing on his mind. He said he'd talk to me after he had peed.

He joined Liz and me at our table for a few minutes when he'd finished upstairs and turned on the charm. Having wheedled my phone number out of me – just before I suggested he take note of it – he left to drink his coffee at another table.

He phoned me that night. I sat on the landing at the top of the staircase as we chatted for an hour. I felt like I was seventeen once more. Within three days we had gone out for coffee, enjoyed a curry dinner and had our first kiss. At our age there is no point in dilly-dallying, especially if there is clear evidence that his plumbing still works.

Being in a relationship at this stage of life is quite different to one enjoyed when younger. We didn't know what how to introduce each other to friends and family for the first few months. I got very peeved when Mike introduced me to his friends as 'Pam, my friend' and then patted me twice on the shoulder to emphasize the point. I wanted to poke his eyes out. It's a wonder we got to the point of even discussing our titles.

'Boyfriend and girlfriend' didn't work as Mike was way beyond being a boy although it suited me as we older women always call our peers 'girls'. 'Partners' was too business-like. 'Lovers' was altogether most unsuitable as we had a reputation to maintain. We also didn't 'go out' as much as stay in. Geriatric dating was a whole new ballgame.

Meeting the families was interesting. Mike met Heather in the pre-school car-park when she was with two friends so both of them were trying too hard to be cool. He met James when he was going through a torrid first marriage. Being Aspergers, James didn't speak very much so Mike spent a lot of time talking and James spent a lot of time grunting depressingly. We drove up to meet Rich and Alan in their Mitcham home in outer London for Mike's first meeting with them. They prepared dinner for us and I don't know who was more anxious. It was like taking my boyfriend to meet my parents. I think he passed the test.

Then it was my turn to meet his kids. They all were mightily worried that I was a weirdo. Sadly, their worries were confirmed but as I was not quite as weird as their own dad, they cut me some slack.

I was taken to the coffee shop where we'd met to meet with Mike's daughter Vicky and her small daughter Zoe. Vicky sussed me out whilst I did my best to be charming and delightful. Meeting his son Patch was like meeting a younger version of Mike, with the addition of tattoos. His soon-to-be wife Kate and their daughter Cloe were warm and welcoming. I was in!

Geriatric love is wonderful. There are so many issues that are no longer important. You don't have to win every argument. You know what you like and what you don't like. It's a love that's relaxed. It's a love that requires you to immediately give him his own den, a man-cave to which he can retreat.

A man-cave should be mandatory for all couples. It's Mike's home for all his really important stuff which would otherwise be in the bedroom. It's space for him to do his Sudoku and to read books. A place to smoke. It's a spot in which he can bond with our kitty-cat, TopDeck. It's a room he can lock so Heather can't nick his tobacco and small change. It's what makes a marriage great.

* * *

Mike had a light-bulb moment one day. He wanted to ride solo to France, Spain and Portugal on a bike or a scooter. There were three problems with this whim that were glaringly apparent. One, he hadn't ridden a bike for forty years. Two, he didn't have a bike. Three, it was nearly winter.

He addressed the first problem by riding a pedal bike to get back into riding a two-wheeler. So we went to a beauty spot on the coast near Eastbourne and hired bikes. I hadn't ridden a bicycle for thirty years and Mike for longer than that. I had to think deeply before I got on the bike. Do I throw my leg over the saddle to mount it? *Could* I throw my leg over the saddle? Then, once on, how do I start forward motion? Would I be able to balance? These were real concerns.

Mike got on his and wobbled his way wildly onto the path that wound its way through wetland towards the sea. I followed, somewhat gingerly, ringing my bell at everyone who was in my way. How we didn't mow people down I'll never know, but eventually I got the hang of it and shot ahead of my beloved, who wasn't quite as nifty a rider as I was. At one point I heard a faint scream and a splash but cycled on regardless, mainly because it was difficult to stop.

A short while later I realised Mike was not behind me so I managed to stop and turn around to look for him. In the distance I saw a waving limb and a wheel sticking out from a river bank and heard what may have been my name being called. Helping a grown man who is wrapped around a bicycle out of a water ditch is very funny if you are the rescuer. It's apparently not funny for the grown man.

This experience somehow convinced Mike to buy a scooter and set off for Europe the very next week. There was little forward thinking involved as winter was about to begin but I waved my hardy lover goodbye and off he set, tootling down the road towards Newhaven on his 50cc, ready to conquer the world.

What he hadn't counted on was the fact that the days were now short and the evenings very long and very cold. He was travelling on a severely restricted budget and banked on using local campsites for overnight stays. However, campsites weren't open because no normal people camped out in the winter. So he slept in bus shelters and on floors and in doorways. Although he enjoyed the riding and quiet moments spent amidst beautiful scenery, he become more and more miserable as the dark, chilly days progressed. The final straw was when he walked into a bollard in a French village and struck his knee so badly his leg swelled up like a bruised balloon.

He was so jolly miserable he messaged me on Facebook and asked me to marry him.

My father had sent me my mother's engagement ring after her death. A solitaire, it was beautifully designed in the 1950s and I wanted to wear it for my own engagement. I needed my mother close.

We married on the 30th January 2014 in the Regency Room at Brighton City Hall.

I wore purple. I also carried a bouquet of dried purple and white Scottish heather. I designed a purple and white three-tier wedding cake that an ex-CAP client of Rich made for us as a gift. I asked Mike to wear a purple tie, much to his horror. It was an exceptionally purple pledging.

The cake was homage to our first meeting. The bottom tier had the word 'vacant' written on it, the second tier had 'engaged' and the final tier read 'taken'. The two figures at the top were figures with crossed legs that were used to indicate male and female on public conveniences. It was so un-classy and it was perfect.

Mike's daughter Vicky and his son Patch organised a surprise for their dad. Mike knew that Matthew, his youngest son, who lived in Johannesburg, would not able to be at the wedding. However, Matt flew over secretly and the other two smuggled him into my house while Mike was out shopping. The shock of seeing Matt there nearly brought on a heart attack but it absolutely made Mike's day.

So we had all six of our children at our wedding. Rich read out our song – Rihanna's 'We found love in a hopeless place' - in a brilliantly funny way as a reading; James gave me away (a little too willingly, I might add) and Heather and Zoe were my bridesmaids. Alan was our witness, Patch was the best man and Matthew helped with filming the ceremony.

I loved my wedding day. My beloved man was so handsome in his suit and purple tie. My silver stiletto shoes were killing me before the ceremony was even finished but my inner Bridezilla won through. I ignored the shoes and focussed on kissing my brand new husband instead.

My friend Pam organised a small reception for us in the Cafe of our church. She did an amazing job of sorting out decorations, photo sets and everything else needed for a celebration. After a couple of hours of genteel partying it was time to go to our hotel. We'd booked the honeymoon suite at The Shelleys Hotel in Lewes, the same beautiful venue where I'd celebrated my 50th birthday party.

Driving to Lewes only took fifteen minutes and I was exhausted after such a full day. I thought it must be way after midnight and there would be no nookie that night because it was so late and this old bird was knackered. We pulled up at the hotel and I checked the time. It was nearly nine o'clock. The early hour gave me such a shock I got a second wind and I am pleased to report that nookie did actually occur.

We had a four-poster bed in a beautifully furnished suite which was very romantic. What wasn't quite so romantic was the fact that the bed was about four feet high. My hips couldn't take the strain of bending over the bed and then lifting each leg at a time to clamber aboard. Also, the counterpane was silky and I couldn't get a grip so once I positioned like a frog I'd slip down the side of the bed and crumple on the carpet. It was not a good look for a honeymoon night.

I ended up having to take a running jump to land on the top. Once I was on there was no way I was coming off until breakfast. So we had to think of ways to pass the time.

We honeymooned in freezing Lewes for the weekend, acting like tourists even though we lived only a hop, skip and a jump away.

Within two weeks I was in scorching Ethiopia.

Ethiopia

This was my second trip to Addis Ababa. Both trips were part of Holland Road Baptist Church's mission outreaches. The first trip took place in January 2011 and this one, in February 2014, was a follow up.

We stayed at a mission house in Addis, a little oasis tucked away from the bustling city streets. We were close enough to walk to a market to buy gifts for folks back home. I bought hand-carved Ethiopian Orthodox crosses, each one individually styled and beautiful in their intricacies. A fun gift was a traditional version of a Johnson's ear bud. It was a tiny silver spoon attached to a fine handle that was used for cleaning wax out of the ear. I got one for Richard but he was not impressed.

My main role both times was to present teacher training to teachers at Joy Academy in Addis. Joy Academy was set up by an Ethiopian woman, Amsala, who recognised the need for excellent, faith-based schooling for local children and got on with the job of creating one. The school had basic amenities, plenty of smiling children and a number of very dedicated teachers.

What I have learned from teaching and training in different parts of the world is that people are the same the world over. Teachers too, have the same needs and frustrations whether they are based in Ulan Bator or in Addis Ababa. I organised training and workshops for the teachers and further training with the school leaders in how to motivate staff. I had to stop myself from packing up my Brighton home and moving to Addis to continue with this work. I thrived on the challenge.

What I didn't thrive on was the utter chaos that is Addis Ababa. It was like Manila on steroids. Driving was a faith journey, every time. There weren't many good roads anyway but where they did exist, no road rules were followed. It was as if the traffic laws were a vague suggestion that one could follow if so inclined. Not many were inclined. Vehicles were in a shocking state of disrepair as parts and new cars were extremely expensive to buy.

Addis is a blend of many cultures, one of them being Italian thanks to Mussolini's five year occupation from 1936-1941. Italian food, especially pizza, is a specialty and pizzerias dotted the lanes and bigger roads like pubs in English towns. The Ethiopian coffee was superb and their coffee ceremonies were a rite of passage for guests. The national dish was called injera, a spongy, sourdough flatbread on which various 'wats' (lentil, bean, meat or vegetable sauces) are placed. You eat this with your right hand, using the injera as a spoon to lift the other ingredients to your mouth. Local custom dictates that as an act of friendship and love, you grab a bit of injera wrapped around a chunk of stew or some vegetables, and pop it into your friend's mouth. I think I prefer receiving a smiling heart-shaped emoji at the end of a text as a sign of love rather than my friend feeding me gloopy food. I think I have become far too British.

During both trips we were taken to the Yod Abyssinia Traditional Food restaurant, a well-known place that serves authentic Ethiopian food and puts on a traditional music and dance show as you eat. The energy of the performers is staggering. One dance necessitates a woman swinging her head in circles faster and faster until her entire head is a blur. I fully expected it to fly off and land on my injera. Another dance was performed by men, who imitated a pneumatic drill at sensational speed. Jackhammers have never been so entertaining. Another dance involved the shoulders being shrugged at various speeds whilst the waist remains still and eyeballs roll. The entertainers picked a couple of people out of the audience to dance this with them. Naturally, my group knew a patsy when they saw one and pointed me out.

Suffice to say, I tried to shrug dance to the best of my ability. I have no idea what my feet were doing and I was definitely at the beginning stages of twerking as my shoulders leapt up and down completely out of time to the music. My breasts did a shrug dance totally at odds with my shoulder shrug dance and I felt a right twit.

My friend Sarah cracked up completely as she watched me lose all my dignity in a public place. I was delighted when she was picked out to dance the next time we were in Ethiopia. How I laughed.

During our first visit in 2011, some of our group went to the Addis Ababa Fistula Hospital to see the work they do for women throughout Ethiopia. The work was started by a couple, Drs Catherine and Reginald Hamlin who were appalled by the state of fistula patients they came across when they started work in Addis in 1959. Quoting from the Catherine Hamlin Fistula Foundation website,

"In Ethiopia, and large parts of Africa and other parts of the world where there are inadequate medical facilities, these women have a difficult, or perhaps an obstructed labour, maybe for days, leading to a stillborn child, which causes a vaginal fistula (a hole) in the bladder, rectum or in the worst cases, in both, leaving them incontinent in one or two respects. It is lifelong, and untreated, the woman becomes an outcast in her society because of her offensive smell.

Because many of our patients endure their condition for years, they are physically unable to undergo the operation until they have had a long period of physiotherapy."

The hospital still continues to provide all-round care for women who suffer from incontinence, physical impairment, shame and marginalisation as a result of having an obstetric fistula. It is one of the finest examples of love in action I have ever come across.

We went out of the city to visit a settlement called Desta Mender in the foothills of the mountains surrounding Addis Ababa. This was a large area incorporating ten houses devoted to aftercare for women who had attended the Addis Ababa Fistula Hospital. These women have chronic long-term injuries and are not able to return to their homes. It was a beautiful, green enclave in the dusty countryside and I felt for the first time since arriving on this trip that I was actually in Africa. Ethiopia is so unlike Southern or Northern Africa but this little piece of land reminded me of home.

At Desta Mender, the emphasis is on rehabilitation, enabling the women to develop skills useful in the community so that they can eventually leave and find permanent work. We ate a light lunch made by some of the women in the shade of a spreading tree. I bought a beautiful scarf from their small shop as a reminder of their bravery.

I took a stroll through a woodland area and was overcome with the strong feeling that Alan was close by. I still missed him and knew he would have loved this part of the world. I wished I had brought his ashes to Desta Mender and laid them at the foot of the trees surrounding me. I spoke to him, my tears falling onto the African soil as the breeze whispered love through the tree tops.

James

My son James was married for only a couple of months when the abuse started in earnest. His bride, a pretty, black-haired girl, had declared her undying love for him from the moment they met. She made him happy and he returned the affection. However, it soon became clear that she was a bruised, broken girl, inwardly destroyed by family members who had abused her for years on end.

A relationship between a broken victim of abuse and an autistic, shy man is a recipe for utter disaster. James was constantly harangued, scolded, manipulated and rejected to the point of complete dejection and depression. He did not have the social and emotional skills to cope so he retreated within himself and accepted the abuse in all its forms. During a particularly bad time James visited me at my house for a couple of days and got ready to have a shower. As he lifted his shirt I saw blue-black bruises all over his back and torso where he'd been beaten.

Shortly after this the marriage tore apart and he was left with nothing of his own at all. During the brief marriage he lost so much weight his bones were visible. He also lost his home, his car, his possessions and his dignity. He became homeless.

Seeing my precious boy in this state was horrid and I wondered if he would be broken forever.

I had not counted on the inner determination and focus of my son. Over the next nine months he got himself a place on the housing rota for homeless people, a mentor to help him navigate the complex journey ahead, a doctor to help him with mental health issues, a car, a delivery driving job and some basic possessions with which to build a new life. He put on weight and looked healthy once more. He also studied at a local college, achieving certificates in Maths,

English and other courses despite his dyslexia. His super-hero power is perseverance.

A while later it became obvious that he had found another. I do a lot of guess-work when I am with James as his communication can be real sketchy and deeply cryptic. Luckily his face is the window to his soul and when he is happy his dimpled smile creases all the way up to his eyes and if happiness is connected to matters of the heart, he blushes. He did a lot of blushing and an awful lot of dimpling before bringing Yvette around to my house with her two small children. He assumed I would gather they were an item.

I had gained two grandchildren through Mike and was now gifted with another two, Alex and Victoria. It's a bit like getting a kitten. Get one and before you know it, you've got three more taking over your lounge. Both of James' step-children take after their mother with their astonishingly long eye-lashes and big, kewpie-doll eyes.

The Ark Pre-school

My friend Pam wanted to leave her position as pre-school manager and become a tutor for Early Years apprentices so asked me if I wanted to apply.

After nearly five years at St Andrew's Community Pre-school I was ready for a new challenge, so I applied for the position and subsequently became the manager of The Ark Pre-school in Portslade, near my home. The Ark is part of the City Coast Church but is a community enterprise open to all.

Taking over a managerial post is interesting. Most people are threatened by change so change had to happen in increments. Trust had to be built between me and the staff as well and that takes time. The parental group we served were completely different to that of my previous school and I needed new approaches. Many of the children in this new school had additional needs, which created a challenging dynamic in the setting. Bridges had to be built between church and pre-school. The to-do list went on and on.

Fund-raising was crucial to my goal of developing our outdoor area into a proper playground. This area was mostly a fenced-off section of a car park and edged with metal security fence railings on one side. Slowly but surely our garden started to transform thanks to events, raffles and grants. Even Mike did his bit in raising money. He wanted to do his second scooter ride to France, Spain and Portugal and combined it with fund-raising for the pre-school. Mike called his venture Little Bike Big Ride.

So we gave him a little teddy bear which the children had decided would be called Barry. Barry Bear was dressed in a T-shirt bearing the school's logo and we asked Mike to take photographs of him as he travelled.

Mike set off for Newhaven to catch the ferry across to France, flanked by two powerful motorbikes serving as a guard of honour. He phut-phutted on his 100cc scooter between these two growling machines all the way to the harbour. When he arrived, Barry Bear had his first photo call, waiting for a ferry at the terminus.

I wonder what the French thought when they saw this elderly gentleman with a backpack on his scooter, enjoying a picnic of baguettes and cheese with Barry. Or what went through Portugese minds when Mike tootled through villages with Barry peering over the handlebars. Or noting Spaniards' reactions when looking at Mike and Barry Bear waiting for breakfast after a good sleep, camped in a little park at Villarquemado on the N234 to Zaragoza.

Mike and Barry Bear had developed a very close relationship by the time they returned home on the very day Mike turned 70.

Managing a pre-school is a complex business. You have to be a multi-tasker and have eyes at the back of your head. It's beneficial to have a knowledge of how to withstand kiddie rugby tackles, avoid paint spattering and being kicked in the teeth and know how to smile when a solid metal bike is driven right over your foot.

You have to be a mental health specialist as staff members, usually women, cope with their own family traumas as well as those at work. You have to remind the male staff member about the distress showing a builder's bum can cause to the fairer sex. She-who-must-be-obeyed, Ofsted, is an ever-lurking presence and standards have to be kept up at all times. Then there's nurturing the parents, dealing with Social Services, Speech and Language and Additional Needs specialists plus keeping up to date with the Local Educational Authority. Then you still have to budget, plan, deliver training, write reports, do appraisals, operate as an employment agency and be fully trained in Paediatric First Aid. On top of that you have to be a theatre producer, putting on a Christmas show every year.

Trying to get children to act in a Nativity Play is such fun - said no-one ever. Arranging the heavenly angelic host is like herding cats. Joseph frequently refuses to hold hands with Mary and the Three

Wise men always rip their gift-wrapped parcels open before they get to Baby Jesus. One year somebody stole Baby Jesus and we only noticed as the cast of knee-highs worshipped a piece of Lego in an empty crib. The children forget to sing so the staff belt out carols cheerfully to fill the awful silence. Every year there are at least three wailers, who then become sobbers, followed by becoming screamers. These little darlings are then plucked from the stage area and deposited into their parents' laps. The smallest and sometimes the most disruptive kids, are dressed as farm animals; cows adorned with tinsel wrestle noisily with lumpy-backed camels as Silent Night is being sung. Tears come to parents' eyes. Tears come to my eyes too but for entirely different reasons.

Our yearly end-of-year Graduation ceremony is similarly challenging. It is like herding mortarboard-wearing cats. Balancing their mortarboards on their heads makes them lose all sense of direction. They weave onto the stage area, looking lost and bewildered. Once seated on their little chairs, they yank their caps over their faces or swing them around like flying saucers. Some sink slowly onto the stage floor from their chairs like a slinky made from over-cooked spaghetti. There is always at least one who yells blue murder and tears around the room with his parents in full pursuit. One or two cry like kittens when they recognise their parents sitting in the front row.

This is a snapshot of the future leaders of the world.

Parents weep. Teachers weep. Children weep. It's a very happy occasion.

Being an ambulance is a useful skill which helps fulfil the manager's role. I have taken a number of staff members to hospital, two very recently. One was bitten in her shoulder by a razor-sharp set of two-year-old chompers and had to have a tetanus injection. The other teacher had a sharp edge of thin cardboard thrust directly into her eye so off we went to the Eye Hospital for treatment. This job needs danger pay. Fortunately I have brilliant staff members, who are hardy and resilient even as they pour out their hearts into their little charges.

Whilst at The Ark I have worked with two administrators, Elaine and Dena. Elaine is a Liverpudlian which means she speaks a whole different language which I have to try and interpret. She has the most generous smile and raucous laugh this side of England. Her go-to phrase in times of work stress was 'Teeth and Tits! Teeth and Tits!' and she'd push her substantial bosom out, bare her beautiful teeth in a cheery smile and get on with life. She worked with me for over four years, being my Scouse comforter and strength during my son's illness and death.

Dena is a bit older than me, I like to point out. We make up the geriatric department. She is the Laurel to my Hardy especially when it comes to techie things. Dena is the size of a pixie and can't reach half of what she needs to at work. When she peers in at the pre-school door window all you can see is blonde curls. She is so elfin that if she is typing on her computer I cannot see her behind her monitor. We bumble through the day, somehow managing to keep the pre-school afloat and functioning.

My current staff members are fabulously diverse. Eve is awesome. She is like a modern-day Mary Poppins, a miracle-working teacher and a walking tattoo-artist's easel. Her favourite saying is, 'it is what it is'. She could run a Master Class on how to teach pre-schoolers and how to handle parents' expectations. She is fire and ice. She is formidable.

Lynsey is our special needs teacher. She is precise, organised, neat and loves a good rota. She is inclined to anxiety and likes to know what will happen in five years time. Change is difficult for her and has to be processed with care. Lynsey prefers routine and simply loves to file stuff. Her files are legendary and shall be donated to a museum of education in the future.

Chloe is our adult apprentice. She is a French-speaking Greek woman in her mid-thirties and achingly chic. She can't help it. She oozes Gallic charm. She speaks English with a sexy French/Greek drawl and often ends a sentence with...eh, non? She brings her little boy to pre-school. He is about a foot high, cute as a button and tri-lingual. They belong in a Tintin annual.

Teacher Danni is like a wild colt, kicking up her heels and whinnying into the cliff-top winds. She has unbridled enthusiasm and no working knowledge of social etiquette whatsoever. Danni frequently watches inappropriate words fly out of her mouth but cannot catch them back quickly enough. She spreads effervescent joy amongst the children and staff.

Michael started working as a one to one key worker last year. He is a mountain of a man, a qualified fitness instructor and a musician. Mike sings almost all day long and refers to his little charge as 'buddy'. He has an innovative approach to teaching. His favourite thing at the moment is using a supermarket delivery crate as a rocket or a sailing boat for his child who loves flying through the air at a cracking speed.

Cherise is another one to one worker. Her own child has ASC (Autistic Spectrum Condition) so she shows such understanding of and patience towards her key child. Despite being bitten regularly by him she knows just how to rock him into blissful contentment and smooth over his frustrations.

My saving grace in bringing the pre-school up to an excellent standard was being introduced to coaching. One couple, Simon and Ruth, who are very involved in the Centre, were qualified coaches and used their skills both privately and within the church to help others. Ruth was assigned to be my coach to help me with my goals as a new manager. We meet once a month and have done so since I started. Coaching changed my life.

I was able to set targets for pre-school and achieve my goals. I was also able to pace the rate of change that was needed and to make sure important issues were dealt with and not just urgent ones. Coaching was my self-appraisal technique. I firmly believe coaching was part of the success of the pre-school in reaching an Outstanding Grade from Ofsted in 2017.

I wanted to learn how to coach. Ruth organised a small group she would train and I joined that group, along with Rich, my money-maestro friend.

I had to practise on two people as part of the coaching qualification. So I nabbed Liz, from my previous pre-school and Elaine, my administrator at the time. Coaching Elaine was a challenge as desired outcomes weren't clear at all in the beginning. However, she responded so well to coaching and gained so much self-belief and focus in the process that she promptly resigned from the pre-school and took up another career. It certainly was an unexpected result for me and it paved the way for dinky Dena to work as my right-hand woman.

Romania

To my delight, I had another opportunity to accompany a mission trip, this time to Romania.

The church to which I belonged at this time, Holland Road Baptist Church, began to form a relationship with a pastor in Romania, thanks to an elderly church member, Margie, who had lived there for a number of years and who had affected the introduction. Margie had been to my previous church and I knew her quite well. She was very well-meaning and a sterling church member but I didn't want to go on a mission with her. She was strident and difficult to work with as part of a team and had very little awareness of personal space. I am so glad I put my personal judgements to one side and followed my heart as Margie was crucial in translating for us, in building good relationships and showing us cultural niceties. She was called Bunica (Grandma) within the church family in Iasi and shown much respect and love by those she had previously lived amongst.

A small team left the church for Heathrow on a cold autumn day. As we flew, snow started falling and it became thicker and thicker as we neared Bucharest. By the time we were thirty minutes out of the city we were flying through a blizzard. Looking out the aeroplane window, I saw only tempestuous swirling white snow. It was like being in a snow-globe. As we prepared for landing, all the passengers and crew fell silent. We couldn't see the land; neither could we see the sky. The pilot brought the plane down in a steady descent and with a deft touch, landed and cruised gently to a halt. Everyone on board clapped and cheered wildly, relieved they were alive to tell the tale. As I was disembarking I asked a cabin crew member to thank the pilot. Thank her yourself, she said with a smile and pointed to the person on her right - a lovely young woman who looked as if she was sixteen. Women drivers really are the best.

We had to wait for a few hours at the airport until the blizzard lifted and we could catch our flight to Iasi which lay near the Moldova border. The plane in which we flew was a small propeller plane and I fleetingly wondered if this was the way in which I was to be called to my heavenly home. I prepared myself for eternity during the flight, just in case.

Romania was another country that had been through a transition. Communism had left its destructive legacy, clear to see by unfinished and abandoned buildings, rows of ugly flats and military-style constructions. Juxtaposed with this were beautiful cathedrals and churches belonging to the Romanian Orthodox church, some pretty parks and many open markets.

Margie and I stayed with the pastor, David and his wife in their flat, a functional three bedroom ground floor unit in a treed area of Iasi. We were treated to excellent dining by the pastor's wife who produced an extraordinary amount of delicious food from her humble kitchen.

Every day we were served some kind of borscht, a sour soup made using a fermented base, also called borscht. A mixture comprising wheat bran, corn bran, water, yeast and rye bread is commonly used to make this unique stock and the cook rings the changes by making the soup with vegetables alone or by adding meat.

Living with a local family showed how Romania was edging ever closer towards the modern, cyber age. I watched Romanian Pop Idol on the telly whilst I was there, as well as programmes that were current in the UK and in the USA. My hosts Skyped their daughter in America every week and most people used smart phones. As in Africa, this was often done amongst terrible poverty and poor infrastructure. Whilst visiting a very poor community outside the city I met several women who lived in abject need and after we chatted, they whipped out their cell phones to add me to their Facebook friends list.

I spoke at a women's meeting in two churches, one in the countryside and one in central Iasi, our base church for the trip. It amazes me how much we women are alike the world over. There is a commonality of spirit, purpose and dreams. There is also universal suffering. I talked with women who were beaten by their husbands, women who were struggling to fall pregnant, women who had put on weight and had lost sense of their own beauty and identity, women who were not married and longed for a husband and women who battled to feed their families due to lack of income. The only thing I could offer them was the love of a Father, who heard their every cry. We bonded over faith, food and fun and I left Romania, richer in spirit than when I'd arrived.

The Club-7 Gay, reunited

There is a page on Facebook that is dedicated to Club 7, the youth club in Rouxville, Johannesburg that had so shaped my life. Once young and naive, most of us are now in our late fifties or over and a lot more knowing about the mysteries of life. At first, connecting with each other was a little disconcerting as we had become our parents but the delight of seeing such loved, if a bit wrinkly, faces from the past is fantastic.

But nobody could find Jay, our beloved token gay, even though some of us had tried to find him for the last thirty-five years.

One busy day, whilst I was working on the computer at work, a Facebook message popped up on the screen from the Club 7 group. It was from a Ben who wanted to know if anyone remembered Jay. I quickly responded and asked how Ben knew Jay. Confusingly, Ben then said he WAS Jay and after a few minutes chatting online I discovered he lived ten minutes drive away from my home in a nearby suburb of Brighton. After thirty-five years of looking for him, I found him in my neighbourhood.

So Jay and I met up in the same cafe bar in which I had met Mike, my husband. The last time I had seen him he was a slight-figured, floppy-haired wraith, with soulful blue eyes and a cheeky grin. We managed to recognise each other only because when I texted him to say I was in the cafe, a middle-aged man with silver hair sitting across from me read a text and looked up, to see me, a middle-aged woman with silver hair, looking down at my phone.

As well as having a non-de-plume on Facebook, Jay does nothing according to the rules if he can possibly help it. He is a Professor of Music, with the title of Doctor preceding his name. He is married to a gentleman and has two children. He also has a property portfolio and has recently moved to one of his previous homes, a country pile in the North, with over two hundred acres of grounds. He is rich. He is a proud Catholic. He is also eccentric and a walking medical marvel.

He has had a brain clot removed, various cancers in diverse parts of his body, organ operations, back trouble and many other ailments. How his skin holds all his chopped innards together I don't know.

Jay and I entertain all old Club 7-ers who happen to pass through or near Brighton. We scream with delight upon seeing old friends and spend hours chatting over the good old days. All of us are wrinkly and have settled into our middle-aged bodies most comfortably. Through our gossipy catch-ups we have discovered that an awful lot of naughty stuff went on behind the scenes at the time. I think it's definitely time for a full Club 7 reunion, grey hair and zimmer frames allowed.

'Anni Horribilis'

On 24 November 1992 The Queen gave a speech at Guildhall to mark the 40th anniversary of her Accession. In it, she referred to recent events as part of an 'annus horribilis'.

'1992 is not a year on which I shall look back with undiluted pleasure. In the words of one of my more sympathetic correspondents, it has turned out to be an 'Annus Horribilis'.

The years between 2015 and 2017 were my 'Anni Horibilis'. My narrative is disjointed, I have memory lapses, I am undone.

Heather

Firstly, I need to devote an entire chapter to Heather, whose behaviour and difficulties run though this time and still go on today. The whirlwind I lived with for the first part of her life became a super-tornado when she was in her teen years and has continued to gather momentum until the present day.

High school and Heather were like opposite magnetic poles. She became the class clown and amused her classmates daily with her antics. The teachers were not quite as amused and she was in detention so regularly she had her own chair set aside. One of her problems was that she could not sit still and listen, or sit and complete a task. She talked as much as she breathed. Other children were constantly distracted by her and she was often sent out of class for disrupting lessons.

Of course, those who were like her gravitated towards her and she became one of the naughty crowd. Heather discovered cigarettes, vodka and weed and loved going to the park with her cool buddies before and after school. The first time she smoked weed, aged fourteen, she got lost as she tried to find the train station and I had to rescue her somewhere in another suburb entirely. She couldn't even stand up straight. She was so out of it I took her to hospital where she was kept for a few hours under observation.

Throwing tantrums was one of her hobbies. She threw spectacular foamies wherever the mood took her. One memorable day we were in Brighton shopping, when she had a hissy fit on the pavement. People were streaming past, whipping their heads around to peer at this fifteen-year-old five-foot-nothing wild child stamping her feet and yelling at her mother. At this point I had enough of her nonsense. So I threw myself onto the pavement, kicking and screaming, tossing my arms around like rotor blades and all in all, threw the most splendid tantrum known to mankind. A crowd gathered. She was mortified. Begging me to stop she helped me to my feet and we tottered down the road arm in arm to a bench, upon which we sat, exhausted.

Heather's fondness for weed and booze continued all through school and it was with a great sense of relief that she actually stayed the course and even managed to attend her Prom night. Rich bought her a beautiful, above-the-knee lacy Hollister dress, white with a blue waist band and bow. Her hair was done in a long weave; she wore sky-high blue high heels and carried a lace and diamante clutch bag. She looked stunning. Her friends and her drove to the Prom in a Hummer and Mike and I took photographs like we were paparazzi.

Heather could not wait for anything. She had no sense of the passing of time at all so every activity or task became stressful. If she was due in town at 2:00pm she'd get ready at 1:50pm and have a meltdown because she was running late. If I was on my way to fetch her from somewhere she would be on the phone, calling me every few minutes to ask where I was. This did awful things to my blood pressure and I usually ended up screaming at her down the phone to stop calling. Her impatience has improved slightly since she started her medication but timing still has to be talked through before any event.

Her list of lost items grows daily. She has lost four passports, her Indefinite Leave to Remain stamp, seven mobile phones and two electronic tablets. She has also lost clothing, handbags, shoes, bus cards, purses and money. She currently has no acceptable form of ID except a birth certificate and certainly no photo ID, without which she cannot apply for benefits, a provisional driving licence or a bank account. Just replacing a passport is a lengthy, expensive business and we have done it four times so far. It requires copious form-filling, a return trip to London (which costs a packet), a day's wait at the South African Home Office, the cost of food and drinks for the day, then a four month wait for the passport to be ready. When it is ready, we then have to go back up to London for another day trip to collect it. Once we have got her next passport I have to pay for her to get another Right to Remain in the UK stamp or card. The stress of it all is relentless.

Spontaneity is a symptom of ADHD and Heather is the queen of unbridled impromptu, impetuous actions. A friend dared her to steal some vodka from a supermarket near us. So she did, entering the store dressed like a gangster, her favoured dress code at the time, sidled over to the booze section and slid a bottle under her hoodie. Naturally she was nabbed as soon as she stepped out of the door.

She studied at College for one year, lasting that long by the narrowest margin. Her time-keeping for classes was dreadful and she became the class clown once again. Her next attempt at a useful life came when she started a personal training and lifeguarding apprenticeship. That lasted a mere few weeks before being asked to leave because of unpunctuality and disappearing when the mood took her.

At one point I was up in Edinburgh, having flown up to see Richard who had recently been diagnosed. I had left Heather at home alone whilst Mike was away on his second scooter trip across Europe. I woke up one morning to read a text on my phone from her. It read, 'Don't worry you'll get your car back.' That is a very odd text to receive and I called her immediately. She had decided to throw a party at my house and had invited all fifty or so of her closest friends. Besides trashing my kitchen and spraying the passage ceiling with coffee and spirits, a few of them chose to go for a joy ride in my car. I had hidden my keys in a safe place but Heather managed to find them and pass them on to her drunken friends. Four of them took my car on a jolly and ended up side-swiping a whole row of cars on the other side of Brighton. My car was a write-off.

I took her to the doctor when I returned from Edinburgh and told him I could no longer cope. She needed help or I needed to emigrate to get away from her destructive behaviour. Within two weeks she was diagnosed with ADHD. This made perfect sense and medication started making a difference in her life and mine. However, bad habits take time to die and she continued with her madcap existence.

Her behaviour drew her towards the bad boys in town. Reckless living combined with alcohol became a way of life for her and it just about did me in. She came home drunk so many times it became the norm. If we locked the front door she'd climb up a wall and enter through the first floor windows. She started selling weed and other drugs to get some money and to fit in with her crowd. Her moment of crowning glory in terms of expanding her drug-selling empire was when she tried to sell drugs to under-cover police officers. Her behaviour was so bad I told her she had to leave home. She was not taking her medication and she had absolutely no measure of self-control.

By that time she'd been arrested numerous times for drinking in a public place, anti-social behaviour, theft, selling weed, hopping trains, affray and a whole litany of other misdemeanours. I had stopped fetching her from custody or attending her court appearances. When she left the house and stayed with friends it got even worse. She had to sell drugs in lieu of rent and she began to be one with the bottom-feeders of Brighton.

We called the police to our home a number of times when Heather tried to break in and once when she destroyed my kitchen door with a single kick. That time it took four policemen to slap handcuffs on her, arrest her and carry her, screaming at the top of her voice, out of the building. There were many incidents of similar ilk and I was worn out with despair.

Every policeman in Brighton knew her by name. She looked terrible. My beautiful daughter lost the spark in her eyes and her reason for being. Finally, she came to my work one day and said she needed to come home. She was now seeing people shoot up heroin and take cocaine simultaneously. She was scared.

Taking her back was the only thing I could do, but there were boundaries put in place by Mike and I. It continues to be a rough ride at times but each good day is a blessing. She has gone through so much and has deep-seated issues to explore; being a trans-racial adoptee, moving to another country, parental divorce, living with extreme ADHD, the death of her dad, her granny, her grandpa and her brother. It is not a light load to bear.

There is only one bubbly, funny, talented Heather in this world and I believe she'll soon find her place and make her mark and I shall be the proudest mother in the world. I shall probably be the most relieved and exhausted mother in the world as well.

I bring to mind the picture of heather growing on the moors, strong, hardy, and holding firm against all the inclement weather. I am reminded that she is a survivor. I just hope to God that I am one too.

Loss

James and Yvette were up to something. They threw funny looks at each other and cracked in-house jokes I didn't understand. They seemed very happy about the mystery secret even though Yvette seemed to be very pale and drawn. It all became clear when they revealed she was sixteen weeks pregnant.

Even before I could process the wonder of a new life, Yvette was rushed to hospital with complications. My boy, James, sat with Yvette throughout labour and they delivered the baby together in a small hospital room. Baby Theo was born sleeping. A fully formed, translucent little miracle, he was laid in a crocheted basket and kept close until Yvette left hospital. Leaving him behind pierced the souls of both mum and dad. All I have of him, my first-born blood grandchild, is a snow-globe containing a scan photograph of Theo, safe and sound in his mother's womb a couple of weeks earlier.

Mike and I accompanied James and Yvette to fetch Theo's little coffin from the undertakers. There are no words to describe the loss and the love we all felt, as they carried his snow-white baby casket to the car. We made our way to the crematorium in silence, tears falling down Theo's parents' cheeks. Once there, we placed him on the altar of the tiny chapel and spoke to him, stroking his name etched onto the coffin and the words below, 'Theodore Wohlers-Bebb, born sleeping. 16th January 2016.'

We honoured him, that day, whispering words of love until the curtain fell and we could see him no more.

This loss was soon followed by another.

My father had been ailing for some time. My mother had been his support and he could not manage without her. He didn't like giving up his independence and moving into a room in the Frail Care Unit at the Golden Harvest Retirement Village in Randburg but he got to the stage of being unable to care adequately for himself. My parents had moved into a lovely three-bedroom unit there over twenty years beforehand but the Frail Care Unit was known as God's Waiting Room.

He began to lose his memory and was prone to hallucinations. He also started losing control of his bodily functions and this handsome, intelligent man began to be a shadow of his former self.

He was admitted to Olivedale Clinic and my brother Peter told me he thought the end was near. So I booked a flight and flew in to Johannesburg in the early hours of the morning on the 12th March 2016. My niece Kathy picked me up from the airport, drove me to her house to drop it off then took us straight to the hospital. I was willing my dad to wait for me, telling him I was coming and I wanted to see him. Praying he would hold on for me. He did not.

Five minutes away from the hospital we got a call saying my dad had died. Walking in to the ward felt surreal. Knowing I had just missed his passing caused sorrow I could not process.

The nurse led me to his room. My dad lay in the curtained-off bed, arms by his side, head tilted backwards. His body was still warm and I stroked his arm, speaking unintelligible words. I kissed his forehead and left the cubicle, closing the curtains behind me.

My sister Jenny arrived a couple of days after me and we joined the rest of the family in working out funeral arrangements. Jen and I stayed with Kathy and her two beautiful, feisty children for the next few weeks. Kathy was in the middle of a divorce battle and had got herself into a terrible physical, mental and emotional state. Just before Jenny arrived, Kathy had a breakdown and I took her to my old psychiatrist's office. I knew Dr McGraw could work his magic. Nothing like keeping it in the family. I really should have asked for commission for the number of people I referred to him.

He sent Kathy to stay in his specialized facility for a month just down the road from her home and Jenny and I were left holding the babies. There is an unalterable fact about death and it's this – life goes on. The more I suffer loss, the clearer the truth of this fact.

Housework still needs to be done. Children need to be fed, bathed and put to bed. Shopping needs to be done. Family get-togethers have to happen. You still have to clip your toenails and Veet under your chin. Nothing changes yet everything changes. Your soul drags along the floor behind you as if to say the journey ahead is too dark and too deep and too difficult to endure.

I left Johannesburg as a middle-aged orphan. Parental ties were now severed and I didn't feel grown up enough to be the matriarch of the family. However, my son was dying back home and I had to try and hold myself intact for a few more months.

Richard

My life was ripped to shreds the year before my father died. My Richard, aged twenty-eight, now living between Edinburgh and London, where he worked as a manager for a designer clothing store, began feeling out of sorts. One day, quite out of the blue, he had a seizure and went to the clinic a day or so afterwards to have himself checked out. It appeared it was related to being dehydrated after working out at the gym. However, the second time it happened, he had a seizure on a bus and was taken to hospital by ambulance.

Alan phoned me from Edinburgh and told me the news. He was unable to get there from such a distance but I knew at once that I should go to him. This time it seemed different. His step-dad and I drove up immediately and found him looking unwell, bemused and exhausted in a crowded emergency ward. He was taken for a brain scan whilst we waited, speaking little, fearing lots. When the nurse came back with the result she said words that cut through spirit, soul and body - there is a mass on your brain - and I heard myself scream within, No! No! No! and I knew life as we all knew it, had ended.

Rich was a big, strong young man, with a heart and a smile that made the world a better place. He started fighting from that point on and would not let us, his family, his husband or his friends, give up the fight at any time either. Watching him go into theatre to have his skull cut open and his mass removed, waiting for news, trying to keep the inner screaming contained ushered us into a different reality, a strange, endless new world of fear and dark secrets, a world with no borders or signposts, no clearly defined roads and many unmarked cul-de-sacs.

Prognosis came about ten days later, after being released from hospital. How do you process a bald statement outlining the fact that this mass was cancerous and life limiting? How do you react when told your child, your husband, your brother, your friend is told he will not survive beyond eighteen months? I saw the shock, fear and horror in my boy's eyes as he tried to take in and absorb this death warrant; I crumbled when he still tried to reassure me with what became his mantra for the next few months...'don't worry Mum, it'll be okay.' As it was, it was far less than eighteen months. And it wasn't okay.

I travelled up to Edinburgh from Brighton many times over the next year. Driving through the beauty of the Scottish borders, whether through swirling snow or late evening summer sunshine, filled me with a sense of the circle of life, a knowing that seasons come and go and each season has its own loveliness. I wanted to hold onto you in the summer of life forever, yet all around us autumnal winds blew, ushering in the cold of winter and the finality of death.

(As I am writing, I find myself talking to Rich, writing to him as I did before. How strange. He seems so close, so I will continue.)

There is one day I will always remember. In-between hospital stays, whilst you were at home, you lay on your bed, Alan beside you on one side, and me, sitting next to you on the other.

When you were a baby and then a toddler, I'd get you to sleep by stroking your forehead, then tracing paths around your eyes with my fingers, ever so gently. You loved that. It was our mother-son love letter written in Braille. Now, as a man, yet feeble as a baby, you wanted me to stroke your forehead and brush my fingers over your eyes once more. You smiled as you closed your eyes and lost yourself in a mother's love.

Hospital memories are a mixture of happy visits from friends and times of extraordinary pain. Once, when I was sitting with you at your bedside, you got up and started walking to the toilet, drip attached. You got there, a little unsteadily and closed the door. The next minute there was a huge bang, the sound of a body falling heavily onto bathroom fixtures. My heart stopped when I heard that sound and I screamed in fear, calling for help. You'd blacked out after a seizure and it took three nurses to extricate you and put you back to bed.

The nursing staff adored you. You made them laugh and you were always so polite, so thankful for anything they did for you. They thought you were so handsome and they particularly loved your teeth! I reckon your teeth had a fan club all for themselves.

Despite all medical procedures you underwent, your cancer had spread its tentacles throughout your brain, hooking into every crevice it could find. You started losing your memory, you started seeing people and things that were not there, you started letting go.

Moving you to the hospice was supremely difficult for me to handle. I knew this would be your last resting place. I cannot even talk to you now, about how desperate I felt, how dreadful it was to see you struggle for breath. You started sleeping for much of the time and all I could do, with Alan, was watch, say I loved you and kiss your closed eyelids. As I wrote to you in my letter below, I couldn't stay to see you take your leave.

And so, you were here, then you were gone. You were my longed-for baby one minute and the next minute you were a man. I expected you to stay. I expected that I would go before you. I expected you to tease me when I was an old codger and to take me for tea at the park of an afternoon. I expected us to laugh together every day of our lives until my false teeth flew out into my tea cup and your laughter cascaded over the scones we shared. I did not expect you to leave me.

I wrote two letters to you, Rich, after you left. It was too hard to say these things using my spoken words.

A Terrible Privilege

To my darling Richard

A good friend of mine, who knows a thing or two about loss, suggested I write a letter to you.

I've been putting it off because it's all just too painful. But here goes.

We spoke about so many things, you and I. We had so many funny conversations – your sense of humour was so sharp and clever and we shared a warped sense of the absurd. We also had many philosophical discourses and often put the world to rights (especially after a glass or two of wine).

When I was low, you usually had stern words for me – short, no-nonsense sentences delivered in a deep, warning tone urging me to buck up my act and look at the positives.

However, you were essentially a very private person. You didn't like other people seeing you down, or struggle, and you hid your times of depression as best as you could. You always wanted to make others feel better.

So, when you became ill, for the most part we talked cheerily and positively and with humour. There were brief moments when we spoke about the hardest things, when we were having coffees in cosy coffee shops in Edinburgh. We spoke about faith and fighting this most awful of battles, about those who had gone before, like your beloved granny and grandpa and your dad. But we couldn't talk like that for long.

As I'm writing this to you, it hits me – I am speaking about you in the past tense. This splinters my soul – and my grief at losing you bursts through the cracks in the paper-thin armour I have erected around my heart.

Our little family was all together around your dad's final place of rest. We were a fractured family, bruised and torn from life's great smorgasbord of experiences; yet we loved each other...and despite all the hurts and misunderstandings, we were gathered around his bed, showing your dad love and supporting him through his last days.

I saw your dad, the man I had loved and lived with for over 24 years, lying frail and worn in the hospice bed; his eyes and gentle smile showed how happy he was to have us all there for his last four days on this earth. Past difficulties meant nothing, the present, the all too brief present, was a gift to be cherished.

I saw him, Rich, I saw him move from this world to the next. I felt his own mum, who had died years before, in the room – you used to call her Little Granny, much to your other gran's chagrin as she, by default, was then Big Granny! His mum was there, waiting to welcome him home. She was more real than the hospice staff, her love was tangible. As your dad breathed ever slower, his breath became ragged and hoarse. We waited, breathlessly, for each laboured sigh as he edged towards eternity.

Then, his next breath didn't come. He slipped away into Little Granny's arms and left this world and its struggles forever.

I saw him, Rich, I saw his face slackened by illness, turn to grey. I saw the life going out of his eyes. I saw the finality of death. I called being with him at the end a terrible privilege. What an honour to be with someone you love when they die...and what a horror.

Your granny, my mum, died a few short years ago. I can't even begin to write about how that feels. Not yet. However, this year in March, your granddad, Poppa, became ill and started to fail. You were ill by then and I was so worried about you that it was hard to fly to South Africa to see him. I talked to him in my head and told him to wait for me, I was coming! After landing in Johannesburg in the morning your cousin Kathy and I went straight to the hospital to see him. Ten minutes away, we received a phone call to say he had passed. He hadn't waited, he'd gone.

I had to see him, Rich. The nurses were still preparing him when we arrived. I walked into the ward, not wanting to open the curtain surrounding his bed, my heart breaking as I took in the silence, the absence of breath, the absence of life. Once inside, I saw him. My precious dad, still warm to the touch, his eyes opened a crack – enough to show there was no light, no life. I stroked his arm and tried to talk to him but my voice sounded strangled and incomprehensible. I just said thank you, thank you, and told him I loved him.

I still haven't really processed his death my boy – you were in my mind and thoughts too much. I'm just glad that you, your grannies and grandpa are all together now – yes, I do believe that – and that brings me a small measure of comfort.

And now I come to the point in my letter that I've been dreading. You see, I had to make a choice when you were leaving this world. Grabbing every opportunity to see you in the last year you had, I cherished each moment but at the same time hated the growing horror (that word again) of the reality of your prognosis.

You moved into the hospice – a place you never wanted to go because you'd seen your dad in one and it was a sign of accepting that death was near. This hospice was beautiful though and you were close to the water and in Edinburgh, a city you loved. Your beloved, Alan, was there all the time and your many friends came to see you so often. There was much laughter and many tears. Towards the end you were quite oblivious to most things around you as you prepared yourself to leave us.

Rich, I saw you. I saw how your breath was getting more ragged and what an effort it was to engage with this life. I saw my son, who I loved with my whole being, disappearing by the moment. And I had to make a choice. Do I stay until you take your last breath? Could I see you like your dad and your grandpa, lifeless, with skin cold and eyes sightless? Could I live with that image seared into my brain? Could I watch you go without my soul being torn in two? I could not.

My darling child, I made the decision to go. To leave your precious husband Alan, who had cared for you so richly and so lovingly during your illness, to stay with you as you departed. He embraced the terrible privilege and he did it with angel's wings.

My tears pour down my face as I write this – I know you would understand and I think you would have told me to go home and not worry, as you usually did – but I want you to know I loved you; even as Alan put the phone to your mouth and I heard your groans over the miles as your body prepared to release your spirit, I whispered my everlasting love and thanks to you.

My darling Richard, I cannot write more. I cannot see through my tears. But I will write again. I want to tell you how your sister received the news in typical Bebb fashion, that is, full of drama and in extraordinarily colourful circumstances. It would have made you laugh it was so absurd!

I miss you. Three little words that say everything and yet say nothing.

Your mum.

Mardi-gras Mourning – A second letter

To my darling Richard

Writing my letter to you last week has taken its toll. It opened my heart and spirit too wide, it exposed the very centre of my being and since then I swing uncontrollably between feeling numb and disconnected to feeling achingly, unutterably broken. Yesterday I went shopping and it was all too much – too many people, too many lights, too much noise, too much choice. I couldn't decide between two varieties of grape; my ability to think shut down and the pressure of choosing one or the other caused me to sob wretchedly at the fruit counter before plodding like an automaton to the checkout, without grapes. Without purpose.

In my first letter to you, I wrote that I would tell you how your sister Heather took the news of your death. So here it is, in brief.

It was the night of Brighton Pride, the 6th August, 2016, when you decided to leave us. You had left your mark on Brighton Pride years ago and one of the pictures I love of you is the one of you, standing on a float, looking beautiful and happy.

I rather think you would have enjoyed the timing of it all. You always said Heather and I were drama queens but you, dear boy, fall right into that category too. Heather thought she would go to the parade and pretend all was well with the help of thousands of her closest friends (you know what she's like!). When we got the final call from Alan, the last fragment of hope dissolved in our tears and the world as we knew it, ended. I can't talk more about that again just yet, so will get on with telling you about Heather.

I phoned to tell her the news and after some time her friend answered the phone. I asked to speak to Heather and she said she couldn't come to the phone right now as she was in the middle of an important conversation. Well! You can imagine my reaction, Rich!

Turned out she was having a conversation with the police (or the Feds, as the pseudo-gang culture peeps in Brighton call them) and was nearly arrested for fighting, which of course she denied. The police refused to let her speak on the phone so I had to wait a while until that was sorted out. Then, as she was given the phone by her friend, she knew without speaking, that you were gone. She screamed and shouted and lost all control – I was sobbing and trying to relay information to no avail. I told her to wait and we would go and fetch her.

Mike and I leapt into the car and drove to central Brighton. Rich, you would remember this – Gay Pride Parade, a seething mass of humanity, clad in all colours of the rainbow, men in eye-wateringly high stiletto heels and outrageous wigs, people fancy-dressed as Superman, Spiderman, Elsa from Frozen and even Bart Simpson, men and women bedecked in feathers and wings and lace and ribbons. The noise shook the city. Gigantic speakers were placed on the pavements and the rhythm rocked and echoed through the streets, bouncing off shop windows and rumbling right through the bones of our bodies.

You would have enjoyed this picture, Rich – your 71 year old step-dad, Mike, dressed in his jeans and tweed cap, parking the car in an illegal spot, right next to speakers ten feet tall. He got out to smoke and was immediately swamped by a raucous group of singing drag queens barrelling their way through the revellers. I found Heather, by some miracle, in amongst her group of friends and we embraced fiercely. I was dressed (by chance) all in black, she was dressed for carnival, and we clutched each other, howling like wild women, keening, wailing, mourning. Encircled by festival goers – 'ooh, so emosh!' one said as he passed, waving a banner – assailed by incessant throbbing music beats and shrieking catcalls and laughter, we cried helplessly for you.

Heather then turned away abruptly and ran through the crowd, unseeing, wild with despair. I couldn't find her, so Mike and I left the festivities and drove back, drained, to a more solemn reality.

So, that was our first night without you on this earth. I wish I knew what it had been like for you, as you left this world and flew into a mardi-gras of immense proportions. The colour! The light! The music! The love!

I had just a glimpse of this glory the following night, when Mike took me to a lonely stretch of Shoreham beach so I could maybe find some salve for my soul. Walking across the pebbles, the night black but lit by moonlight, I wept as I talked with you…you were closer to me than a whisper that night, I could almost feel your breath on my cheek as my heart burned within me. I felt your presence strongly, so loving, and so knowing. After a while of communing with you, I turned, my back towards the sea, ready to go home, when I saw this…a crowd of angelic beings, some strangely familiar to me, all dressed in white with powerful wings at rest. They shone with peace and understanding, a curve of heavenly figures on the pebble beach and then, there you were, smiling, in the middle of this 'great crowd of witnesses', surrounded by love.

There are no words to describe my emotions at that point, Rich. What I was seeing was incomprehensible and yet, it was as real to me as the pebbles were under my feet. Tears flowed freely. Joy mixed with the depth of sorrow. Thankfulness and pain.

How I love you, my boy! There are days when I don't know if I can carry on. There are moments of such darkness, I am consumed. And yet, the sun came up this morning, so life, this New Normal, continues and carries me with it.

Rest well, my angel-child. I will write again.

* * *

I never did write to you again, it was simply too painful.

Losing a child is the ultimate grief. It is unnatural, unexpected and impossible to process.

Alan held his Richard's funeral service in Edinburgh, as autumn colours began painting the city in bronze, gold and the darkest of reds. He was surrounded by friends at this final farewell and we, his family, were carried by their love. Rich had asked for everyone to wear blue – Blue for Bebb - so there was a sea of blue in the little chapel. After the service we threw flowers in the Firth of Forth, said our own prayers, thought about this beautiful boy and shared funny memories of our times with Rich with each other.

As there were many people who lived down in the south of the England that could not make the Scottish funeral, I held a memorial service for Rich at City Coast Church, where I worked. Rich and Alan's close friend, Jason, a university lecturer, led the eulogy. It was hysterically funny, quite rude - laced with gay references - and deeply offensive to some. It was perfect, despite seeing the pastor wiping his sweating brow during more lurid moments of the speech. We watched a short video, celebrating Rich from when he was born until he became ill. It made me laugh and cry as his gorgeous smile lit up the giant screen. I have to say, Rich had the best wedding and the best memorial ever. I like to think he was present, laughing with us and drying our tears, as we remembered him.

Above all, I will never forget the love and support the gay community showed towards Rich and towards his family. The hugs and the help we received were beyond anything we could have asked for. I think there is a special place in heaven for those who, like these friends, love others extravagantly.

Time spent with Rich until the day he left us forever may be told later in other stories that I remember with great delight, broken heartedness and bewilderment. Dealing with his death and his absence will take longer. Right now I am angry, lost, hurt, broken. I am not big and strong and brave like he was. I am not inspired to raise money for cancer victims, to console others going through the same thing. I am not pretending I am fine. I am not.

Richard's husband Alan was advised that this, the post-Richard world, was the New Normal. It's a good phrase. It's neither positive nor negative. It makes no promises. It just is.

But I don't know how to live in this New Normal. At the moment I chug along, tears pouring like rain, shouting silently at Richard - why did you leave me? - and start each day as if I am walking through black, sticky treacle.

And so, I walk on, askew, somewhat blinded by grief, feeling my way. A mother lost.

There are the 'firsts' that need to be endured. The first Christmas. The first New Year. The first birthday. The first Mother's Day. They come thick and fast, like battering rams to the heart.

The first Christmas was especially hard. I felt desolate. I hung a blue sequinned bauble for Richard on our Christmas tree (which I only put up on Christmas Eve solely for the benefit of my grandchildren). The bauble was placed at the top, near the star, and Richard's photograph was on the wall just to the side of it.

Did it help? Not really. Mostly my grief burned fiercely within me, behind a facsimile of a festive face, whilst the reflections of sparkly Christmassy lights danced on the edges of my vision, exacerbating the darkness within my soul.

I had some dramatic moments in the days leading up to Christmas. Nearly passing out in busy, loud supermarkets which boomed out tinny seasonal songs was a favourite response of mine. All the faux cheer and overabundance of all things Christmassy was too much.

My butchery is located at the corner shops near me so I thought I could handle going in to buy some distinctly un-festive steak mince. Now my butcher is a large man, at least 6.3ft tall and just about as wide. He is a Northerner so always delivers a bucket-load of friendliness whilst phrases such as 'yes, me love!' echo around the walls of the shop. I waited my turn, feeling more and more fragile as time went on (shopping was, and still is, really hard for me to do) until he turned to me and asked, grinning his enormous happy smile, if I had ordered my Christmas meat hamper. At which point my insides crumbled, my heart scrunched and tears shot out of my eyes like I'd tapped into a bottomless geyser. 'I'm not ordering!' I sobbed through my teeth and tears, 'because my son has just died!' and stood, quivering helplessly in the middle of the butchery, surrounded by stunned customers and assorted meats adorned with frilly festive red and green ribbons.

My burly butcher put down the order he was working on and marched around the counter, wiping his bloody hands on his apron, then, wrapping his huge arms around me, he whispered comfort whilst holding me upright at the same time. I never did buy the mince, never mind a turkey. But my towering Geordie butcher was my own personal bloody Christmas fairy.

When it was time to acknowledge that 2017 had arrived and that living had to carry on, I had to find a way in my head of surviving. One day, after a particularly difficult period of wanting to join my boy rather than be here without him, I had an epiphany. It dawned on me that I could live today, I could actually manage that, because if I lived today, then it was one day closer to when I'd see him again. Our reunion is moving forward, one day by one day, and I could make that time count.

I try to remember that now, as the date of his second death anniversary draws near and the circle of life continues. However, it is not always possible.

Some days are Richard days. I reckon anyone who is acquainted with grief will recognize these times. These are days when I construct my own cathedral around me once again. There are no lucky bean trees here, in the South of England, no blood-red spiky blooms to cast a stained-glass glow, no coral beads with ends dipped in black to make an offering to grief. The best I can do is to go to Shoreham beach, where I saw Richard surrounded by angelic beings on the night after his death. There, I keen into the salty wind and let my tears flow.

I never know when these days will strike. I have to wonder, was it because he was in my dreams that night? - a laughing twelve-year old opening the front door telling me he was home. Maybe it's because looking at old photos stirred up memories. It could just be because I'm resting and life's urgencies aren't forming a shield around my heart, breaching my defences. Sometimes it's just a song, or a joke or a phrase in a book that strips my heart bare in an instant and the will to live leaks right through the soles of my feet, leaving me empty and devoid of hope.

Oh, for just a moment with him…

Making memories

In the meantime, I have two children who need love and a clutch of grandchildren, with whom I need to make memories. Richard is tucked into my heart and I carry him with me, so he is part of the on-going story.

Amelia

James and Yvette broke the news of the impending arrival of my new grandchild by showing me a doctor's letter confirming a pre-natal appointment. I could not contain my joy. To have new life after so much sorrow was like a message from heaven.

Yvette spent the next nine months vomiting, at times in hospital on drips and at other times in her bed, covers drawn over her head. She was growing a particularly ravenous human who sucked everything out of her. I was not told the baby's gender before she was born and I was just as happy to be grandma either to an Arthur or a Martha.

All baby's birth plans were organised, a little bag was packed and Braxton-Hicks contractions bravely borne. It was arranged that I babysit the two older children whilst they went to the hospital when it was time for the birth.

What do they say about plans? As Robbie Burns wrote, 'The best laid schemes o' mice an' men Gang aft a-gley, [*often go awry*]. Indeed. Swap guinea pigs for mice and the plans still go awry.

My ring-tone woke me up at ten minutes to midnight. Baby was coming! My babysitting services for Alex and Victoria were called for so I shot out of bed, threw a coat on and drove like a maniac down the motorway.

James and Yvette were both in the lounge and it was plain to see and hear that advanced labour had begun. Yvette was climbing the back of the sofa groaning and screaming whilst James pottered around being helpful. Very quickly contractions came thick and fast, about a minute apart and there was no way they were going to make the hospital.

James called the midwives who were busy elsewhere. They cheerfully said they'd be there as soon as they could, which was not what we needed to hear. At that point James threw a single mattress down on the floor, covered it with black bin bags and wedged it between the television, the sofa, a chair and a cage of three puzzled guinea pigs. We had an audience.

It was time to whip off the pyjama trousers and get down to business. It's not the side of a daughter-in-law one generally gets to see. I guess having one's mother-in-law peer at one's bulging nether regions isn't common either. James got the emergency team on the phone because the midwives were lost and couldn't find us.

Following instructions relayed over the phone I acted as a pukka midwife whilst James tended to his beloved's every need. At one stage I leaned over and stroked her arm and whispered encouraging words of love. She repaid my administrations by growling DO. NOT. TOUCH. ME. GET. OFF! through clenched jaws, her crazed demonic eyes shining brightly.

It was time. Baby wanted to greet the guinea pigs and nothing was going to stop her. Her head started emerging and I realised then why men faint when watching their partners giving birth. I had never seen childbirth from this end and I will forever salute all rear-end birthing partners for their bravery.

The head was out. Disembodied, and entirely unimpressed, she looked at me. Now what? She seemed to say. I didn't know. I hadn't realised that the head would just sit there for a while and assess the situation. I felt like formally introducing myself. The guinea pigs were equally uncertain of polite protocol.

Just as her shoulders squeezed out, the midwives arrived, threw down a plastic mat and caught the baby. Amelia Barbara Wohlers-Bebb had made her entrance to this world.

I drove home slowly just as the blue-grey dawn was breaking. There wasn't another car on the motorway and through the open windows I could hear birdsong, a swelling chorus of praise that heralded the arrival of Amelia. The earth was rejoicing. I whispered love to my angel-baby, my boy, my man-child, my Rich, as the warm breeze carried the exultation into a new day.

Carry on Caravanning

My step-daughter Vicky asked me to take Zoe away for the February half-term. Zoe had been getting into trouble at school for months and she had been hard work at home too. She couldn't be trusted to spend loads of time with friends back home during the holidays whilst her mum worked so I agreed to have her. To make this week extra-special fun, Heather had to come too as I couldn't trust her at home either. The two girls are ten years apart in age but on the same exact level of sassy crabbiness.

So Vicky booked us a static caravan in a caravan resort near Poole. We arrived at this tiny box on bricks just as the weather turned icy and rainy. There was one bedroom, which I nabbed and a living area that contained a fold-away double bed. The advert had said it was cosy. What they didn't mention was the fact that this caravan was right against the main road and at night time it sounded like the Grand Prix.

The girls tried to put the double bed up in the sitting area. It was like watching the Two Ronnies. Their communication level was the same as in the famous Four Candles skit and they ended up very hot and bothered and practically entangled in the bed springs before giving up and choosing to sleep on the hard lounge seats. I would not recommend them to help anyone with assembling Ikea purchases.

We explored the park in-between rain showers, swam in the indoor pool and watched the evening entertainment, which mainly consisted of second-rate acts belting out Eighties music or magicians whose magic powers magically eluded them during their act. Each evening's entertainment was preceded by a disco. For two nights the girls sat glum-faced in the dark, glaring at the other holiday-makers dancing. They were too cool to dance. Heather was cross because I would not buy her alcohol. Zoe was cross because I would not buy her food. I was cross because they were being right royal pains in the butt. I decide the only way out of this holiday misery was to embarrass them, so I stood up and started granny-dancing.

If there's one worse thing than not getting what you want, it's seeing your mother or grandmother doing all the moves to YMCA. On a chair. Right next to you. In public. They promised they would go and dance on the dance floor if I stopped doing my solo impression of the Village People. I agreed and they shot off to shake their booty to the beat. Frankly I was very relieved as my back had gone out on 'I was down and out with the blues…' and doing the hand movements was becoming a little awkward.

I continued my theme of embarrassment at the Splashdown Waterpark in Poole.

The waterpark had lots of flumes and tubes and water spouts in which one could frolic. The girls encouraged me to ride the biggest flume with them. Tube riding a giant flume and being supersonically ejected at the final pool is fabulous when one is young. However, just getting onto the tube was my first challenge. I attempted to lodge myself into the giant tube numerous times, the queue behind me getting ever more interested in my ridiculous failures.

Heather eventually hauled me up and on and the rapids instantly sped me away to the first pool. I turned head over heels more times than I could count, much to the delight of the crowded balcony of spectators. Once in this pool I could not re-mount the pink inflatable for love or money despite my tubby middle-aged efforts, two girls heaving my flailing body amidst the rapids and an ever-increasing number of encouraging supporters.

I thought I'd drown when I clunked my head on the flume wall but rallied to finally jam my rear end into the tube before hurtling towards oblivion. My screams echoed through the long and windy pitch-black tunnel of doom and I was spat out at speed, limbs akimbo, into the final pool. With all the swimmers watching I was so happy I was wearing my very fetching Disney Mickey Mouse costume with modesty skirt.

I draped myself over the pool steps to catch my breath before heaving myself out of the pool and repairing to the coffee shop section which faced me. It was then I realised that every other silver-haired person in the joint was sitting drinking a hot beverage and doing their crossword puzzles. None of them were in the water, getting tumbled as if in a washing machine. I really must start acting my age sometime soon.

Aging

There are days I come home from work and I collapse onto my bed like a stupefied starfish. Sheer exhaustion drains the life out of me and I remain spread-eagled on my bed until I make dinner. I simply cannot do what I used to do without a great deal of tiredness and an ever-increasing level of bodily aches and pains. Getting older is interesting, in a queer sort of way.

I see my mother's hands emerging from my sleeves now. It's always a bit of a shock. I have developed the dreaded bingo wings I have heard so much about. Facial beauty spots have trebled in number and are now called age spots. My arm skin is crêpey. My eyebrows have travelled south and now reside comfortably under my chin. There is a gum disease war going on in my mouth and the gaps between my teeth can hold enough food for later, in case I get hungry.

Menopause struck when I was forty three. Although I had always been a fairly gentle soul, especially as anti-depressants were another food group in my diet, I started feeling as taut as a trip-wire. I developed my mother's skill of eliminating others by using only one's eyeballs as assassination tools. Speaking one syllable at a time through clenched teeth was also most effective when others were annoying. Crying became a pastime. I cried at adverts on telly for cystitis. I cried when soap opera characters fell in love. I cried if a stranger was nice to me in the shops. I cried because I cried so much.

Physically, my body gave up the fight against gravity. I sagged. I had to buy Veet by the tub, as shaving under my chin was leaving me with bristly after-five shadow. From plucking the life out of my eyebrows I now had to find them and fill them in with Brunette Brow Brush. My Aunty no longer visited terribly much which was a blessing but when she did, she overstayed her welcome with a vengeance. Women really have to put up with a lot in this regard. Menopausal periods are grim. Going out at these times necessitated a packing of one's hind quarters with treble-thick layers of protection and carrying a bulky hold-all containing all kinds of stuffing materials with which one could plug the flow during the day. The pain was excruciating as I felt my womb lining peeling away, month after month.

Eventually I saw a gynaecologist at the hospital who read my notes and suggested that in order to know more she would have to get a piece of my womb out and send it for examination. That sounded like a good plan. I didn't mind being put to sleep next week or even next month, whatever would suit the doctor. 'Great!' she said, then told me to come into the room next door, whip off my knickers and jump onto a chair that looked like a torture device. I obeyed, in a daze. This was to happen now? A nurse came along and took hold of my hand as I lay back in the reclining chair. She looked at me sadly and gave my hand a little squeeze. Another nurse came in and hiked my legs into the air and put my feet into stirrups. Now, as I have previously explained, I don't really do horse riding of any kind, particularly not when on my back in front of strangers. I don't think there is any other position in the world that is quite as helpless and exposed.

Peering through my sight-line between my knees, I saw the doctor approaching with the dreaded speculum. There are times when a Wikipedia definition is called for. It reads like this. 'A vaginal speculum, developed by J. Marion Sims, consists of a hollow cylinder with a rounded end that is divided into two hinged parts, somewhat like the beak of a duck.'

I have two questions for J. Marion Sims. One, why would a beak of a duck make you think 'ah, that's what will open vaginas nicely!' and two, what other creatures inspired this invention before settling on a duck?

At any rate, duck-bill was going in and opening wide. All good so far. This is something a female gets used to during her lifetime although it is never pleasant. Once I was evincing enough of a yawn, like Edvard Munch's character in 'The Scream', she stopped her twisting of the speculum and fetched her next piece of equipment.

This was a foot-long steel object with a pair of tiny scissors on the end. They looked so cute. Until they started approaching. 'Mind the Gap!' would have been an appropriate response from me but I was speechless, struck dumb in horror. This pair of scissors was inserted right up until the cervix got in the way. I would have thought the doctor knew cervixes existed but she gave no sign she knew about such things. Ploughing on regardless, she thrust the scissors right into my womb and snipped a bit, before hooking a lump of flesh out of me and waving it triumphantly in the air. I nearly fainted. My sad nurse squeezed my hand tighter.

Just as I was coming around from nearly passing out and started thinking about getting up from the stirrups, the doctor examined the sample, screwing her eyes up as she did so. 'Hmmm' she said, 'this is a bit small. I shall have to do this again. Open wide!' And she did do it again and I swore it was with obvious enjoyment.

No menopause is complete without hot flushes. Every window in the house had to be open. I placed a fan next to me when I worked on the computer or when I watched telly. I trolled the chiller aisles in supermarkets. I self-combusted randomly. At any given moment my face turned bright scarlet and beads of sweat formed, geyser-like, on my forehead and my cheeks. My hair dripped with salty sweat. I considered moving into an industrial fridge for the duration of this transition. I never knew this transition would last over fifteen years. As I near sixty, these flushes are at last dissipating. They will not be missed.

As I continue to age, hair-dyeing has become a thing of the past. When I walk past a shop window and catch sight of my reflection I wonder who that woman is. Talking about hair reminds me about my latest fall which I had at my hairdresser's salon. Falling is horrible when you are an adult, especially when you are fairly advanced in years.

After putting my handbag down on the floor next to my chair, I sat down and discussed options with my hairdresser, Sophie. Hair options are pretty restricted, to be truthful, as I cannot afford the upkeep of dyeing my hair and regularly touching up the roots. Silver is the new grey, I like to think. Sophie always has a giggle when she sees me for a cut as my hair loses all control a week before the appointment. I am a silver, curly-haired Marge Simpson. After she'd finished chuckling and patting my bouncy fur-ball she asked me to go to the wash basins on the other side of the salon.

I leapt up from the chair and started striding quickly across the room. Unfortunately, in my eagerness I didn't notice that my feet were caught up in the handles of my bag until I felt myself flying through the air. In my mind I fell in slow motion, arms swinging uselessly as I crashed to the floor like a giant redwood. Face down, I considered my next move. I decided to cry. I am not a pretty crier. My face turns to putty and my belly shakes and I sound like a vixen on heat. Sophie and her fellow hairdressers, all under the age of thirty, rallied around, turned me over and administered first aid. My left knee had split open, showing pulpy flesh oozing out and my right knee and elbows were grazed. Once they had patched me up we faced the next problem. I had to get up off the floor.

I cannot get off the floor at the best of times. My knees are still damaged from coming down Mt Snowdon so I have to get on all fours before arising from any floor. Now I couldn't even do that as my knees were completely out of action. So, as an audience watched, Sophie and her manager gripped me under my arms and in a show of amazing strength and commitment, hauled me upright. I cried some more. Wordlessly, Sophie dry-cut my hair as I slumped low in the chair with my legs up on a stool.

This fall reminds me that aging has also brought me another love relationship. This one involves an inanimate object and I simply cannot go anywhere without it...just in case. I am talking about Foldup Canvas Chair That Lives in the Car Boot. My pet name for this is simply, Chair.

Chair and I are inseparable when it comes to outdoor activities. The older I get, the more difficult it is to plop on the floor or the grass or the beach or on park-land. Actually, I'm pretty good at plopping, it's just the getting up I can no longer manage with ease or with grace. Rising off a grassy knoll is immeasurably embarrassing and I challenge my inner giraffe as I stoop down, arms wide open, hands spread wide on the grass, bum up, legs adrift, as if I were drinking from an African waterhole. There is a next step to the waterhole pose and that entails a lifting of the head and a firm, business-like push-off from ground-zero. If the push lacks conviction, I drink from the waterhole once more. A successful push-off results in me standing with legs asunder, my arms whipping around in the air, assisting me in gaining my balance. Chair often comes to my rescue mid-push-off, giving me purchase to complete my move. I can depend on Chair.

Mind you, Chair could not have helped me the other day, when Mike and I went for a walk in a wild land area that turned into a three hour trek. We set off at 7:00pm on a summer's evening to have a squizz at the Knepp Estate, a conservation area in the countryside. As I drove, Mike tried to set the SatNav. He didn't have the co-ordinates so he entered the name of the estate under Points of Interest. The computer didn't compute. Mike tried countless times with no success. It didn't help that he had to take his non-reading glasses off so he could look at the SatNav close up whilst I was hurtling us down bumpy countryside lanes. He was getting a little irate so I suggested he use the voice command. It went something like this.

What is your destination? (calm BBC-style male voice)

Knepp Estates. *(controlled Colonial male voice)*

The United States. Is that correct?

No. *(resets device)*

What is your destination? (calm BBC-style male voice)

K-n-e pp EsTATES. *(slightly frazzled Colonial male voice)*

Kewnip tate. Is that correct? (calm BBC-style male voice)

NO! *(resets device, fingers jabbing crossly at said device)*

What is your destination? (calm BBC-style male voice)

KNEPP ESSSTAAATES. *(Colonial face contorted. Every. Single. Letter. Enunciated. Furiously.)*

Neppishates. Is that correct? (calm BBC-style male voice)

FUCK OFF! *(Colonial now blue in face and in language)*

Pardon? *(calm BBC-style male voice)*

Despite a near fatality due to his sky-high blood pressure I cackled hysterically all the way to Knepp Estates, wiping the tears away from my eyes so I could see the road. Who knew a Satnav responded politely to verbal abuse?

When we actually got there, we were enthralled by the wild land. There was such an African feel to the flora and the boiling hot English summer sun was a very good facsimile of an African afternoon sun. As we were only there to see what it all entailed so we could visit at a later date, I wore sandals and carried just a water bottle and a map. We strolled through the glamping grounds, which had scattered yurts and shepherd's huts tucked in amongst the woods and grass lands. We then decided to walk through the fields and forests to the first tree house which, we were told, was very doable within the hour. We presumed that meant there and back. We were wrong.

Just before finding the tree house we saw a couple coming towards us, the first humans we had seen on our walk. The man had a camera that was so huge it hung from his neck and swung below his knees. I said I felt really intimidated by his camera, at which point he whipped out another long lens and said only now was he fully extended. Double entendres flew in the forest air and we soon discovered he was South African and he had a lamb potjie cooking over a fire in his campsite and would we join them for dinner. To put it into perspective, this was equivalent to bumping into a Zulu warrior in the fish aisle in Waitrose as he was choosing his sushi dinner. It was bizarre. So we introduced ourselves properly and waved Keith and Julie goodbye before trying to find the nearest tree house.

We began to get a little worried as dusk fell and two hours passed. The map was rudimentary and as it became darker we could hardly read it at all. The track was hideously uneven due to little rainfall and we had no idea if we were on the right path or not. Graceful fallow deer with enormous antlers glided right past us in the deepening gloom and little red deer sprung off into the forest as we neared them. Giant Longhorn cattle bellowed their greetings as we walked silently by and rabbits hopped alongside until disappearing into the forest verges. It was like a story-book scene. I almost expected Snow White to appear, singing to all the forest creatures.

As night fell, my ankle turned over repeatedly as I negotiated he tricky terrain and a little bit of panic set in. My ankle hurt and I started to imagine the air ambulance hovering above, ready to extricate us from the wilds, if they managed to find us at all. Just then, through the warm, evening haze, we came across a yurt surrounded by yogis, who were chanting eerily in unison. We slunk past and found the path in the now pitch-dark forest leading to Keith and Julie's wigwam where we were welcomed by the rich aroma of slow-cooked lamb.

As I get older, people treat me differently. Sometimes they treat me like I am soft in the head or hard of hearing. Often, I am called 'dear' by shopkeepers or bus drivers and the twenty-year-old dental hygienist scolds me for not using inter-dental sticks correctly. Sometimes I feel like yelling out loud – I'm still sixteen inside! – but if I did succumb to that temptation folk will just think I'm senile.

I have even become a cat lady. Only the one cat will do – my Scottish kitty TopDeck, who is aging alongside me. TopDeck has also become attached to Mike, as if with Velcro. He follows him like a puppy, engaging with Mike in full conversation. He also greets him at the door when he comes home from work and sits on Mike's tummy every night when he sits in his armchair. He has a long chat in the mornings with the usurped Lord of the Manor who serves him Yeo Valley yogurt for breakfast. In the evening he stalks around the bed, waiting until I lay on my side. He then perches on top of my hip and settles in for the night. He is a manipulative little bugger and is in complete control of our affections. I resonate with the late Diana, Princess of Wales, who once said that 'there were three of us in this marriage, so it was a bit crowded'. Camilla had nothing on TopDeck.

Despite the emotional hold pets have on us, they should be compulsory for older people. They work better than antidepressants and blood thinners ever could. Think how much the NHS would save by prescribing kitten therapy for the elderly instead of warfarin. Instead of going to the pharmacy once a month pensioners could visit their local Cat Café for a cup of tea and a cholesterol-free cuddle.

It's very disturbing to think that even if all goes well, I have less time ahead of me on this earth than I have already lived. The one positive with this is the belief I'll see my boy again but other than that, I am disconcerted. Life is shorter with each passing day. I want to grab life and run with its glorious possibilities but grabbing and running is tricky when your bones are getting old and arthritis chews at your knuckles.

Faith, hope and love

Now three things remain; faith, hope and love and the greatest of these is love.
1 Corinthians 13:13

Writing a memoir is an interesting exercise. The story is unfinished, the protagonists are not fully constructed, there is uncertainty ahead.

Knowing what and who to include in one's writings is troublesome. Some events are buried deep and need to stay buried. Other stories need to be written but they may hurt or bring division. Some people I love with all my heart have not been mentioned or have been mentioned just in passing. This is not a true reflection of their abiding influence in my life.

I have not written much about my siblings and their families – I have a brilliantly bonkers extended family that deserves a book in their own right. They probably think this omission is a good thing!

What I have done is go behind my own eyes once more. This is some of my life as I have seen it and it reflects the above three things; faith, hope and love.

Faith has been a part of my life since I was three. My perception of God has changed throughout my life and living a life of faith has a very different meaning to me now than when I was young.

Experiences shape our view of the divine. After my season of abuse at the hands of a predatory paedophile as a young girl, a deep belief that I was worth nothing settled within me. Sometimes, when I sat on the rockery under the shade of the lucky bean tree in Bulawayo, I recited a kind of mantra to myself and to the creatures hiding amongst the stones. 'God only loves boys, He doesn't like girls' - I mumbled in a monotone, over and over until I felt the universe understood.

When my father called me a clumsy oaf or shouted at me when I could not understand my maths homework, it fed my worthlessness. If I disappointed my mother it was only to be expected. I searched for affirmations of my worthlessness throughout the first part of my life. I was not good enough. That was the truth.

Getting to know God takes a lifetime. My faith journey has led me through every man-made denomination imaginable. I have been taught Biblical truth by those who interpreted the Bible literally, with no thought to culture or context. I have been part of spiritual movements that laid down laws that destroyed the vulnerable and addled the brains of the uninformed. I have emerged, broken, from being spiritually disciplined by proud and arrogant leaders. However, I have also been touched by people who radiate grace and love; ordinary people who put their pet peeves to one side and love unconditionally. Much like God, I believe.

God's grace was the truth. It has taken me years to open my mind and realize that God is bigger than church creeds, more noble than religious titles and far less concerned with outward appearances than a whole lot of His followers. I have found Him to be wholly inclusive and full of love.

This gives me hope. Hope for a world where judgment does not precede acceptance. A hope that I will eventually manage to discard my own prejudices and stop focusing on things that are of no importance.

And what about love?

Love is like a lucky bean tree – it is both beautiful and toxic. Lucky beans are also called love beans, prayer beans or rosary beans, a sign that there is more to this world, an acknowledgement that beyond a crimson cathedral there is a promise of more. However, eaten in their natural state, lucky beans and their leaves are poisonous, their toxicity hidden behind their beauty.

As with love; I have learned that love is beautiful, kind, warm and uplifting. I have also learned that love can be hard, soul-destroying and wearying beyond measure.

Love does not equal loss, but it allows for it. I now know that the very deepest pain is felt when we lose a person we love. A well-known quote, attributed to the reigning Queen Elizabeth, says that grief is the price of love.

To put that into context, this thought was initially written by Dr Colin Murray Parkes in his book, Bereavement: Studies of Grief in Adult Life.

"The pain of grief is just as much part of life as the joy of love: it is perhaps the price we pay for love, the cost of commitment. To ignore this fact, or to pretend that it is not so, is to put on emotional blinkers which leave us unprepared for the losses that will inevitably occur in our own lives and unprepared to help others cope with losses in theirs."

Despite the pain and pure exhaustion love demands, love still remains the greatest thing.

Mind you, a chilled jug of Pimms on a hot summer's day comes a close second.